KONDURU · STRUCTURE AND INTEGRATION
IN A SOUTH INDIAN VILLAGE

KONDURU

Structure and Integration in a
South Indian Village

Paul G. Hiebert

UNIVERSITY OF MINNESOTA PRESS

Minneapolis

Library of Congress Catalog Card Number: 75-120-809

ISBN 0-8166-0593-9

FOREWORD

SINCE Sir Henry Maine, a century ago, first wrote on the Indian village community, the veil of mystery surrounding the life and society of the man living in the Indian countryside has been gradually lifted. Much has been written of India by travelers, adventurers, novelists, seekers of mystic truth, missionaries, soldiers, administrators, and scholars. Romance and glamour, sensation and prejudice have colored popular writing about the great subcontinent. In spite of the early start by Maine, objective scholarship by Westerners to counterbalance the unreliable general literature that predominated in the English language has until recently been quite rare.

During the past twenty-five years, we have seen changes and developments in the field of Indic studies, not only in India, Britain, and France, but especially in the United States where prior to World War II barely a handful of scholars was concerned with India. The earlier historians, philosophers, and students of Indian literature have now been joined by social scientists from all fields. Many have been caught up in technical aid programs in which their efforts have engaged them in the fearsome battle against famine and epidemic. Many other social scientists are involved in assisting Indian efforts to build new political machinery for a newly self-governing democracy, to provide education for the hundreds of millions, and to wed Western science with Hindu and Muslim thought. Yet if technical assistance programs are to succeed without bringing unwitting damage to the society being "assisted," it is imperative to know the inner fabric of that society.

Although the city has an increasingly important place in the life of India, the country town and village are still its warp and woof. Here is where the vast majority of India's half billion people live out their lives. Here is where anthropologists are making their special contribution to the understanding of India. The anthropologist's unique approach is the study of whole societies as integrated systems. This makes it possible for him to perceive the intricate structural organization of the Indian little community as a node in the vast system of caste that separates India into cross-cutting, rank-ordered, and mutually interdependent segments which interlace to form a firm and functioning whole.

Konduru is, in my view, a truly fine anthropological exposition of the centuries-old social structure of a south Indian village trembling on the verge of modernization. The complexity of that order is almost inconceivable to the American who thinks of farm communities in terms of the simple homogeneity of the American rural town. Konduru and its satellite hamlets present India in microcosm. Eighty-four caste groups are (1965) represented among its two thousand, nine hundred and sixty-five inhabitants!

Professor Hiebert writes of "the cultural variety among the people jostling each other in the narrow marketplace: ornamented gypsies, scantily clad tribesmen, veiled Muslim women, sari-draped Hindus, and young men in Western-style clothing [who] mingle together creating a colorful array." He presents fascinating "trouble cases" of intra- and inter-caste disputes, which show how the people actually press against, are constrained by, and sometimes modify the system. He writes clearly and always interestingly. But above all he writes informatively, for he brings to his task the intimate knowledge and emotion of one who was born and spent his early life in India, combined with the intellectual objectivity and analytical tools of the modern social anthropologist. With him the reader is carried into the "feel" of the culture, but he also learns to see it as no insider, native to the village or its environs, can. He can see it as a dynamic whole with all its parts simultaneously interacting, illumined by the best of the modern theory of social anthropology.

One does not have to be a specialist to enjoy and derive satisfaction from *Konduru*. Indeed, the general reader with the least curiosity about the ways of his fellow men should find himself irresistibly drawn through the book. The complexities of kinship, caste, and inherited roles in the network of economic, religious, and social services are not instantaneously understandable. Yet Professor Hiebert limns them so clearly that understanding is readily achieved.

Certainly, this book is a must for anyone who presumes to lend a helping hand in inducing cultural change anywhere in Asia, be he agricultural expert, engineer, public health specialist, educator, missionary, diplomat, or member of the Peace Corps. It is in no sense a technician's handbook, but it is a manual of enlightenment.

E. ADAMSON HOEBEL
Regents Professor of Anthropology
University of Minnesota

PREFACE

THE fieldwork on which this study is based extended from 1963 through 1965, after I had acquired fluency in Telugu, the major language of the region. During the first year a survey was made of the general patterns of culture and communication on the plateau and Konduru, the dominant village in the region, was chosen for further investigation. Intensive fieldwork in the village was begun in January 1964 and continued to the end of 1965.

Among the many people, both in India and the United States, to whom I owe a real debt of gratitude, there are a few without whose assistance this research would have been impossible. Professors E. Adamson Hoebel and Robert F. Spencer of the University of Minnesota opened the door for me to the exciting field of anthropology and provided invaluable guidance and criticism throughout the research and writing of this monograph. Rama Chari, Muggayya, Patabi, Jeevarathnam, Tsakali Sayyana, and many others undertook the difficult task of teaching me how to live properly in the village. Professor J. E. Schwartzberg kindly reviewed the manuscript and offered many constructive criticisms. Nellie Aberle, Joan Sorenson, and Phyllis Martens spent long hours editing and typing the manuscript. I would also like to express my appreciation to the Foreign Area Fellowship Program, whose support made this research possible, and to the Kansas State University Bureau of General Research for assistance in getting the manuscript in publishable form. In the end, however, the responsibility for the ideas expressed is my own.

Finally, I want to thank my wife Frances and my children who not only bore patiently the hardships of field research but also contributed very much to the success of the project.

CONTENTS

Photographs between pages 34 and 35

KONDURU · STRUCTURE AND INTEGRATION
IN A SOUTH INDIAN VILLAGE

CHAPTER ONE

SEASONS AND SETTING

THE rolling plains south and west of Hyderabad in the central part of southern India are broken here and there by occasional rock-capped hills. As one nears the Krishna River, a low range of forested hills called the Nallamalais rises above the plains and flanks the river on either side (see Figure 1). Along the northern edge of the river, wedged between the Krishna and its tributary, the Dindi, the hills form a series of stepped plateaus ascending in a southward direction until the range is broken by the deep gorge through which the Krishna cuts its passage to the sea. The first escarpment rises sharply six hundred feet to an elevation of about two thousand feet. Successive lesser escarpments bring the maximum elevation to twenty-eight hundred feet near the forest station of Farahbad.

Most of the Nallamalais are covered with a reserve forest of secondary-stand deciduous trees, bamboo, and creepers. Besides wild boar, deer, peacocks, a few tigers, and other game, the only permanent residents of this wooded area are the forest Chenchu tribe described by Fürer-Haimendorf in his monograph *The Chenchu* (1943). Along the northern edge, however, in a small valley that winds along the top of the first plateau, village life has existed over the past centuries (see Figure 2). Here villages and their surrounding hamlets seem to rise imperceptibly above the mud and rock from which they have been constructed.

The largest and most important village on the plateau is Konduru, a center of trade, government, and cultural activities. Here is held the only weekly market of the region, drawing crowds each Wednesday

3

1. Map of Southern India

from the surrounding villages for trade and visiting. Here live the wealthy merchants who make loans, operate larger shops, buy up cash crops for export, and import goods from the outside. The government offices that provide services for the area are located here: the police headquarters, the hospital, the post office, and the forest ranger station. A new high school draws students from the elementary and middle schools of the plateau.

Konduru is also the center of religion and entertainment. People from nearby villages gather in its temple for the annual marriage festival of the god Rama. Passing bards and drama troupes, which frequent the village, retell the great epic tales of Hindu mythology. Muslims of the plateau gather twice a year to pray at the large prayer wall (*edga*) on the edge of Konduru and to attend services in its mosque.

Around the village, within a radius of three miles, are thirteen small hamlets that are considered part of Konduru. Some consist of a single clean or unclean caste residing alone, while others are made up of farmers living near their lands together with their servants and laborers. These hamlets elect members to the Konduru village council, are

all subject to the same revenue and government officials, and, with one
or two exceptions, have no shops or trade centers of their own.

East of Konduru, at the lower end of the valley, lie four smaller
agricultural villages with their associated hamlets. Podur and Rameshvaram, villages with long histories, are six miles northeast of Konduru,
beyond a low ridge of hills. The villages of Lalapur and Tartikol lie
to the southeast. Beyond these four villages, agriculture ceases and the
forest reserve stretches twenty-five miles to the Krishna and Dindi,
broken only on the eastern edge by two small forest hamlets.

At the head of the valley, six miles west of Konduru, is the village
of Maradpur straddling the junction where a small forest road leaves
the main road and winds into the upper forest plateaus. Maradpur is
the trade center for outside contractors and laborers who exploit such
forest products as teak and bamboo. Until recent times only a few

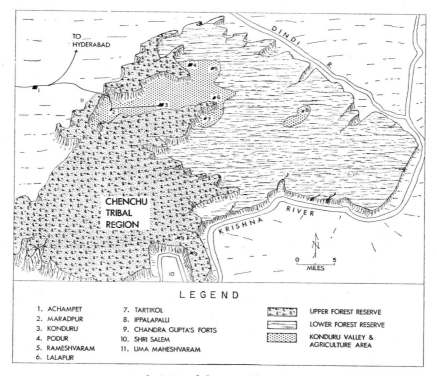

LEGEND

1. ACHAMPET
2. MARADPUR
3. KONDURU
4. PODUR
5. RAMESHVARAM
6. LALAPUR
7. TARTIKOL
8. IPPALAPALLI
9. CHANDRA GUPTA'S FORTS
10. SHRI SALEM
11. UMA MAHESHVARAM

UPPER FOREST RESERVE
LOWER FOREST RESERVE
KONDURU VALLEY & AGRICULTURE AREA

2. Map of the area of study

poor pilgrims came by each spring on their way to the great Shiva temple at Shri Salem, on the banks of the Krishna forty miles to the south. However, a graded road that was opened through the forest in 1965 to carry materials for the construction of a large dam across the Krishna resulted in a considerable increase in traffic across the end of the valley.

The only motorable road to the plateau comes from Achampet, a market town fifteen miles away on the plains. The road winds up a short ghat through a gap in the hills at Maradpur, and runs to its end, six miles down the center of the valley at Konduru. Regular bus service connects these two villages with the outside world except when flooded streams block the roads for a few days or weeks. Trucks come and go, particularly at harvesttime, taking cash crops either to the large market at Jadcherla, sixty-five miles away on the railroad line, or to the large metropolis of Hyderabad, one hundred miles north. They return with drums of kerosene, sacks of grain and salt, and manufactured products such as cigarettes, flashlights, safety pins, paper, pencils, pens, ink, soaps, lamps, and cooking vessels, which are sold in the small general shops by village merchants. Occasional government jeeps pass by on inspection tours; however, for most, travel involves only short distances and is made with oxcarts or by foot.

Beyond Konduru, the road becomes a series of cart trails winding through the valley and over the low hills to surrounding villages. During the dry season, these tracks multiply through the fields where the going is easy, but during the rainy season when the fields are again under cultivation, traffic returns to the old permanent trails between the fields that are badly rutted and difficult to traverse even with oxcarts.

SEASONS

The climate of the area is divided into three major seasons. In late May and early June, the southwest monsoons set in. Heavy rains soften the dry land, making it possible for the farmers to till the soil with their pairs of oxen and iron-tipped plows. As soon as the first rain stops, the farmers are out preparing and seeding the land to gain the maximum benefits from the full monsoon. There is, however, a measure of calculated risk, for these rains may be only premonsoon showers, or the monsoon may be delayed after the first rains and the small seedlings will then suffer serious drought damage. The first to be planted are the kharif crops, the dry-soil crops raised during the rainy season, such as jowar, peanuts, sesame, bajra, chilies, castor beans, and cotton. By July the small tanks or reservoirs, formed by small earthen dams and found every few miles along a stream bed, begin to fill, and the wells rise. The small patches of irrigated land below the tanks and beside large wells are seeded for the first or abi rice crops. By August and September, the tanks are often full to over-flowing. After each rain streams swell, cutting off bus and motor traffic from the outside world, and cart tracks become hard to use. With the coming of the monsoons, daytime temperatures drop from highs above one hundred degrees to the eighties and nineties. Nights are comfortable with temperatures ranging in the seventies (see Table 1).

Table 1. Temperatures (T.) and Mean Rainfall by Months in the Konduru Region

Seasons	Max T.	Min T.	Mean T.	Mean Humidity	Rainfall (in.)
Work season					
SW monsoon					
June 101		69	85.2	69	4.89
July	93	69	80.3	78	5.77
August	92	70	79.1	79	4.05
September	93	70	79.4	78	6.87
October	94	64	79.3	69	5.50
November	89	57	74.5	62	.60
Cold season					
December	88	50	71.1	62	.17
January	91	58	72.6	62	.34
February	91	57	77.1	54	.96
Social season					
Hot season					
March 100		62	83.6	47	.30
April 108		64	88.9	47	1.33
May 110		72	91.2	50	1.59
Total mean annual rainfall					32.47

Rains during the months of October and November when the monsoons retreat become more sporadic. Peanuts, bajra, and sesame are harvested, and some midseason crops, such as linseed and gram, which require less water, are planted. If the original kharif crops are ruined by drought or washout, a farmer may reseed his fields at this time. Although the rains begin to fall less frequently, the already full tanks will overflow with any sizable downpour, which may cause flooding and occasionally the breaching of a tank. This occurred in 1964 when the earthen dam near Maradpur broke and the surging waters washed out the two dams near Konduru. In such an event low-lying crops are flooded, lands irrigated by these tanks are left dry, and the small streams below dry up in summer. Then washermen and herdsmen must go afield for water for their laundries and cattle.

The cold season sets in by late November. Days are cool and nights are cold. People sleep indoors; the poor rise before dawn to ward off the predawn chill by warming themselves beside small fires or by activity. This season is the time for completing the harvest of kharif and late abi crops, for selling chilies, for purchasing clothes with cash, and for celebrating with relatives the great festivals of Divali and Ugadi. The fortunate few having irrigable lands and the initiative to exploit them plant the tabi or spring rices and an occasional vegetable garden.

By February temperatures begin to climb, and the hot season begins. There is little field work; hence, time is spent in mending tools and implements. A few farmers toil early and late, drawing water with their oxen from large open wells for their irrigated crops. For all it is the social period of the year. People are freed from the demanding agricultural work of the monsoon season, and the nights are no longer uncomfortable. There are great fairs to attend at various shrines. All-night dramas are staged in the village square by local youths. Bards, puppeteers, and drama troupes perform in the marketplace. Many activities take place during the cool nights, with the weary participants and spectators sleeping during the heat of the next day. The hot season is considered the auspicious time to arrange marriages and to visit relatives. Only the rich can afford to have marriages performed during other months of the year.

The hot, dry days are occasionally broken by rolling thunderstorms known as the mango showers because they come when the mango trees are in bloom. Villagers believe that these showers come after the great festival of Shivaratri to wash away the filth which camping pilgrims leave on the rocky flats around the Shri Salem temple. With the showers there may be lightning which can strike a village or home. For a few hours after each rain, farmers appear in their fields to break the crusted soil baked by the hot sun.

The cycles of nature leave their imprint upon life in Konduru. Even the cycles of the moon become important in the absence of electricity. A great deal of travel and activity takes place when there is a full moon, but during the new moon, people with no light except a burning wick spend their nights behind the mud walls of their courtyards and homes.

HISTORICAL SETTING

Konduru has two histories. One is told by the old men of the village and reenacted by the village youths in all-night street dramas. In this history no sharp boundaries divide life into discrete categories such as gods, men, and animals. Life in all its manifest forms interacts: men become gods and gods become men, and animals live in a world which mirrors that of human beings. The history of Konduru as told by the villagers is more than a history; it is a cosmology.

Konduru's second history is extracted by contemporary historians from ancient documents and rock inscriptions which are scattered around the countryside. Two crumbling forts in the forests south of Konduru, known locally as Chandra Gupta's forts, possibly date back to the fourth century. Another near the head of the valley is ascribed to Prataparudra of the Kākatīya kingdom who ruled from Warangal at the beginning of the fourteenth century. Numerous megalithic chambers, rock circles, and Stone Age sites indicate an earlier residence of man on the Konduru plateau.

The earliest rock inscription on the plateau is found near the Konduru temple and dates back to 1248. Already, the village was the seat of one of the numerous petty kingdoms that checkered the countryside. The local chieftain bore the title *mahāsāmanta*, great vassal, and ruled as far as Kammamet on the plains below. He apparently belonged to the Viryala dynasty. In inscriptions after 1264, the petty kings are called the Immadis. Two of them, Vishrāntha Devi and Bollayya Reddi, gave extensive gifts to the dynastic god Immadi Deva and to the now nonexistent temples dedicated to Svayambhu, Maitāra, and Mahālakshmi. Mention is also made of the construction of extensive irrigation systems and of at least one vassal subject to the Konduru ruler. From local inscriptions it is clear that the rulers of this area were subject to the Kākatīya kings who governed the eastern Deccan until the fourteenth century. The local lords, however, constantly fought petty wars among themselves to gain power and prestige.

Little is known of Konduru after the fall of the Kākatīya empire to the Muslims. To the north lay the Muslim kingdom of the Bahmanīs while to the south stretched the Hindu empire of Vijayanagar. The Nallamalai hills, east of the great plains where these kingdoms fought innumerable battles, were apparently spared the devastations of war. By 1468 Maradpur at the head of the valley, ruled by the lords of the Nadipita *gōtra*, had gained ascendancy over the plateau. Also, little is known about Konduru during the Golconda kingdom of the Qutb Shāhī dynasty. Between 1687 and 1707, Aurangzeb, the Mughal emperor from Delhi, invaded the Deccan, destroying the Hindu temples as he went. It was probably at this time that the ancient temple in Konduru was destroyed and that the present mosque was constructed from the broken fragments of its finely carved rocks. Numerous headless images in the village are a testimony to the thoroughness of this iconoclastic scourge.

With the passing of Aurangzeb, the first of the Nizams carved out a kingdom in the central Deccan which became known as Hyderabad. Like the previous Muslim state, Hyderabad State was a conglomerate of state lands, privately ruled jagirs, and vassal kingdoms. Adventurers from the Arabian lands came seeking their fortunes. A fortunate few gained the Nizam's favor and were granted jagirs; the rest had to eke out meager livelihoods in the cities and villages, such as Konduru.

The next glimpse of the plateau comes from an old document recording the gift of a field to the Rama temple by Sanjēva Dharma Rao, ruler of Konduru. The document seems to indicate that this lord, a member of the Velama farmer caste, came to Konduru as a zamindar from Deverakonda in the eighteenth century. Local tales of the Washerman, Barber, and Leatherworker castes all tell of their coming to Konduru with such a lord about six or seven generations ago. The document also notes that Venkat Dharma Rao, grandson to Sanjēva, was defeated by the zamindar of Siddāpur on the nearby plains and that the victor destroyed the forts of Konduru and Podur together with the old land records. It was Sanjēva Dharma Rao II, son of the defeated lord, who, with the fallen lords of Podur and Rameshvaram, drove out the usurper and wrote the document renewing the land grant his great-grandfather had made.

The end of these village kingdoms on the plateau is not clear. According to one local tradition, a bitter conflict took place between the plateau lords and the Velama lord of Wanaparty, forty miles to the east, in which the former were defeated, their families and servants slain, and the bodies thrown into the large royal well in the middle of Konduru. There, even now, villagers claim to see piles of bleached bones on the bottom of the well. A second story states that the Nizam's army marched in during the fighting and annexed the petty kingdoms.

Shortly after 1841, the plateau was granted by the Nizam as a military jagir, or fief, to an Arab, Mahmed Budhar Khan. Hyderabad State had degenerated rapidly. The deficit budgets that resulted caused the government to fall into the hands of its ruthless creditors, who were mainly Arab and Persian moneylenders. To repay the loans the Nizam granted revenue rights over certain territories to the creditors. Other portions, including Konduru, were granted as military jagirs to men who raised troops for the Nizam's army.

Matters took a turn for the better when Salar Jung I was appointed prime minister of Hyderabad in 1865. Being an able administrator, he initiated a series of rapid reforms, balanced the budget, and, by paying off the debts, recovered the lands ceded to the moneylenders and military leaders. In 1880, Konduru and the plateau were reclaimed and placed under the direct administration of the central Hyderabad State government (Ali 1885 II, 178). Salar Jung also instituted the division of the state into districts and *tasils*, appointed administrators, and initiated statewide systems of police, courts, hospitals, schools, and taxation, all of which had been lacking up to this time. Roads and railroads were built. The extension of a motorable road to the plateau after the turn of the century opened the plateau to increased communication with the outside world. Until then, the only access had been by trails and a cart track winding up the hills from the northeast.

Shortly after India gained its independence in 1947, Hyderabad State was merged with the new nation. Anti-Muslim reactions swept the plateau for a brief time and some Muslim leaders fled to Hyderabad, but the local Muslim populace suffered little or no harm. For a time Communist bands sought refuge in the nearby forests and came periodically to the villages demanding food and shelter. A few of the wealthy traders migrated to the city for safety. Only after the Indian government liquidated these gangs did peace return to the area.

Several observations emerge from a study of the history of Konduru. First, village life on the plateau has persisted over a long period of time amid famines, plagues, conquests, and wars without the centralized services of a powerful state government. Basic needs seem to have been met by the village itself and by the small kingdoms of which it was a part. Second, lines of political cleavage ran along territorial rather than social boundaries. Fragmentation into tiers of small kingdoms competing for dominance over each other appears to have been the rule despite the broad networks of social and economic ties running across the countryside. Finally, status hierarchy played a key role in politics as well as in the social order. Political rank was expressed through elaborate systems of symbolism based upon conquest, courts, and titles. Knowledge of village stability, the system of petty states, and status rivalry helps in an understanding of the Konduru of today.

CHAPTER TWO

SOCIETAL CATEGORIES

A FOREIGNER visiting Konduru for the first time is struck by the cultural variety among the people jostling each other in the narrow marketplace: ornamented gypsies, scantily clad tribesmen, veiled Muslim women, sari-draped Hindus, turbaned farmers, and young men in Western-style clothing mingle together creating a colorful array. These differences are more than surface phenomena: they reflect the deep-seated social cleavages which underlie the apparent unity of the village and fragment it into numerous social groups. To live in the village each man must belong to one or more of these groups, for as farmer Kortayya said out of bitter experience, "Without castemen and kinsmen to support him, a man is as good as dead. No one will marry him; no one will help him in times of trouble; no one will complete his karma when he dies."

Two things must be understood for the cultural variety in the village to make sense: the social structure — the different kinds of groups in which the villager participates — and the patterns of behavior which relate people to each other, for ordered behavior is considered proper and in it the villager feels at ease.

SOCIAL UNITS

The considerable confusion concerning the nature of social units in India arises partly from the multiplicity of social units and partly from a failure to differentiate between societal categories and social groups. Societal categories, as defined by Bierstedt (1963:294–97), are composed of people who are aware of the similarity or identity of certain traits or characteristics that they all possess. In short, they share a "consciousness of kind." Unlike social groups, however, they are not characterized by social interaction and social organization. Societal categories provide people with a mental image of their social order. Social groups, on the other hand, form the basis for social behavior. They are composed of groups of people who actually associate with one another in social interaction ranging from simple mutual awareness to relationships of the most intimate nature.

Some social units in the Indian social order are clearly societal categories. An example is varna, the religious schema placing all men within a fourfold hierarchy: Brahmans or priests, Kshatriya or warriors, Vaishya or merchants, and Shudra or workers. Theoretically, at least, every caste and every man has a place in this order, which is the same throughout the country. In practice, as we shall see later, the articulation of the societal categories and social groups is often inexact.

Confusion centers around certain social units called *jātis*, which can be seen either as societal categories or as social groups, depending upon the viewpoint. *Jātis*, or castes, as they will be referred to hereafter, have two dimensions. In their broad dimension they are societal categories linking together people of different regions who share certain characteristics. As such, however, they lack clear boundaries, definable organization, or even face-to-face relations between all or most of their members. In their local dimension within the context of the village, castes form the basis upon which many of the social groups are formed. Some of the current confusion about the nature of caste can be avoided by distinguishing clearly between the two views of caste.

Various attempts have been made to define all castes as societal categories by using one or more cultural traits as the definitive criteria: endogamy (Ketkar, Dutt, Karvey), hereditary membership (Ketkar, Senart), occupational monopoly (Risley), ranking (Dutt, Karvey), political entity (Senart), common name (Risley), and ritually determined relationships with other castes (Hutton, Dutt, Senart) have all been suggested. Exceptions can, however, be pointed out for each of these criteria. Some castes have endogamous subunits and others practice hypergamy, a practice whereby women from one caste marry men from castes above them. Hereditary membership, generally thought to be the rule, does not hold for castes, such as the Konduru Courtesans, that previously recruited from other castes. Not all castes have occupational monopolies, and two or more may share the same work rights. Traditionally caste organizations have operated, for the most part, only within small territorial units, which are the maximum expression of the caste as a social group. Only in recent times has there been a trend toward "unionization" of castes on a broader scale into corporate bodies.

Hutton (1946:5) catches the significance of caste when he defines it in terms of a caste system; there is no caste apart from other castes. Within the system each caste as a societal category is a distinct subculture and its members share a consciousness of kind symbolized by a caste name. Cultural distinctives frequently include occupational monopolies, caste deities, and unique customs. That castes are indeed subcultures can be seen in the ferocity with which they guard their cultural distinctives from adoption by others. Imitation by one caste of another's monopoly, such as the right to wear a peacock feather in the hair or to play a certain type of musical instrument, is a frequent cause for village riots. It is the caste system that articulates these castes into a single social order without destroying their cultural distinctives by means of structural interdependence and ordered interaction.

Castes as societal categories must be differentiated from classes. Both are subcultures within broader societies; both may be arranged along a hierarchical scale, and both are initially recruited by birth. Unlike the class structure, however, caste systems lack individual mobility across caste lines except in certain specific situations, and then the change is formally noted. Mobility in the total framework of society is more a function of the caste or a segment of a caste than of the individual. Hindu mythology has many stories of men who tried to pass themselves off as members of higher castes, only to inevitably betray themselves by some cultural shibboleth.

A second difference between classes and castes is that castes are also social groups. While classes provide the general mental framework into which numerous social groups are fitted, in practice they lack a concrete identity in terms of clearly defined boundaries and distinct memberships. Castes, however, are the basis for the formation of mutually exclusive social groups. In the village, membership in caste groups is readily defined and interaction within and between caste groups is easily observed. Caste groups are generally linked with similar groups in surrounding villages to form regional caste groups which have their own autonomy and leadership. But the organization of caste rarely proceeds beyond this point. In its broadest scope, a caste is made up of an indeterminate number of localized caste groups that share certain traits and a consciousness of kind, but may have only tenuous or nonexistent relationships between them. Caste groups in one area may doubt the genuineness of their fellow castemen in other areas; furthermore, the same caste may rank high in one region and low in another.

Castes should also be differentiated from tribes. As Bailey points out (1960:264–65), the difference is not one of kind, but of degree. Caste and tribe occupy the poles of a continuum. Both are endogamous; both usually have exogamous subgroups; both are named; and both have a "we feeling." Their differences lie in their relationships with other peoples. Tribes are independent groups generally having a territorial monopoly, an egalitarian outlook, and a lack of economic specialization. Castes, being at the other end of the scale, are articulated into a heterogeneous society with other castes in the same territory as distinct subcultures between which mobility exists in terms of the castes rather than in terms of individuals.

The similarities between tribes and castes explain the ease with which tribes and migrants are assimilated by a village. Konduru, itself, illustrates the various stages in the process. The Forest Chenchus live as a tribe in the surrounding forests, but increasingly their contacts with Konduru make them dependent upon village culture. The Village Chenchus have moved out of the forest to camp beside one of Konduru's hamlets, but they still construct the round thatch huts unique to the Chenchu and weave and sell the small baskets which were their forest specialty. But now they also join other villagers as day laborers in the fields. Without losing their cultural identity, they are becoming a part of the village and its networks.

Castes may be divided into endogamous subcastes. Unlike castes, subcastes within a caste are not culturally distinct. Their primary role is the regulation of matters within the caste, such as marriage. Members of one caste are often unaware of these divisions in other castes. Karve (1961), seeking to eliminate the need for the term subcaste, equates caste with the endogamous groups. This approach fails to consider that it is not the endogamous unit, but the culturally defined unit, which is significant in village level relations. It is the caste with its cultural and occupational distinctives that is the minimal unit of interaction on the level of the village.

Castes may also be linked together into loose clusters. Castes of a single cluster frequently share a common generic name, common mythical origins, some cultural distinctives, and a sense of brotherhood. An example is the artisan caste cluster known as the Panchalas, which includes the Goldsmith, Brass-smith, Ironsmith, Carpenter, and Rocksmith castes. As will be evident later, in Konduru these castes are set off from the other castes in many ways.

One more type of societal category should be noted, namely *gōtras*. A *gōtra* is an exogamous patrilineal unit within a caste whose members claim descent from one of the ancient rishis or sages within the Brahmanic tradition. In Konduru *gōtras* are functional only among the Brahmans, Vaishyas, and Panchalas. Some Shudra castes have taken on *gōtra* names without following their functions. Thus, for instance, the Konduru Winetappers have only a single *gōtra* in their caste. Among most lower castes, the exogamous groups are *inte pērlu* or house names — named patrilineages. The patrilineages are traceable only as far as memory goes. Migration frequently gives rise to new founders since ties to distant places are soon forgotten.

RESIDENT CASTES

The caste system is striking in its extreme fragmentation. Even a casual survey of the extensive catalogues of castes within the country reveals thousands of them. Those represented in any given region constitute only a fraction of the total.

Eighty-four castes were identified on the Konduru plateau (see Appendix I). Forty-three of these were permanent residents of the area, the rest were transient castes whose members frequented the plateau. Transient castemen often have residential villages elsewhere where they own land and homes. When the crops are in, they leave the aged at home and tour the countryside as beggars, entertainers, mendicants, priests, craftsmen, and salesmen. Others are fully transient, living their whole lives in small bands that migrate from camp to camp according to available work.

Resident castes form the basis for village organization. Two major rifts cut through their ranks and divide the village into four gross communities (see Figure 3). Religion separates Hindus from Muslims and Christians, and ritual purity divides the clean castes from the untouchables. Of these communities, only the clean Hindu castes fit into

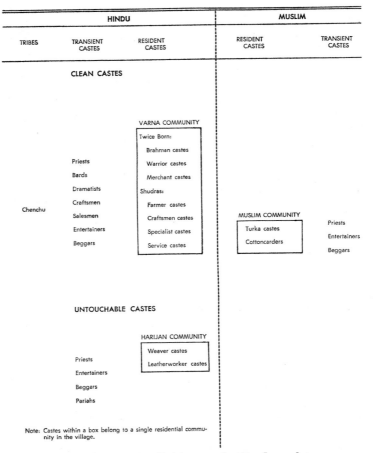

	HINDU			MUSLIM	
TRIBES	TRANSIENT CASTES	RESIDENT CASTES		RESIDENT CASTES	TRANSIENT CASTES

CLEAN CASTES

VARNA COMMUNITY

Twice Born:

Brahman castes

Priests / Warrior castes

Bards / Merchant castes

Dramatists / Shudras:

Craftsmen / Farmer castes

Chenchu

Salesmen / Craftsmen castes   MUSLIM COMMUNITY   Priests

Entertainers / Specialist castes   Turka castes   Entertainers

Beggars / Service castes   Cottoncarders   Beggars

UNTOUCHABLE CASTES

HARIJAN COMMUNITY

Weaver castes

Priests

Leatherworker castes

Entertainers

Beggars

Pariahs

Note: Castes within a box belong to a single residential community in the village.

3. Major community divisions on the Konduru plateau

the varna scheme. They form the core of the village structure. Near them are the clean Muslims, who are a minority. The untouchables are set apart. No untouchable Muslims were observed in Konduru, but their presence was reported on the adjacent plains. Some untouchables in Konduru and its hamlets have become Christians and have formed a separate religious community; but, for the most part, they have retained many of their social ties with their Hindu counterparts.

Hindu Varna Castes

Thirty Hindu castes within the varna scheme form the core around which Konduru and the neighboring villages are built. The highest rank belongs to the three Brahman castes which have the hereditary rights of providing religious services in the village. Smarthulu Brahmans serve as *purohits* or family priests officiating at rituals in the home. Since they are worshipers of both Shiva and Vishnu, they may serve worshipers of either sect. Smarthulu serve also as the village astrologers, who calculate auspicious times for all important undertakings. The Ayyavaru Brahmans of Konduru originally came from a Kanarese-speaking area two hundred miles to the south. Known also as Shri Vaishnavas because they follow the precepts of the sage Ramanujacharya, the Konduru Ayyavaru serve as hereditary priests in the Rama temple; however, they rank lower than the Smarthulu, for temple priests are thought of as servants to the devotees who come to worship. The Konduru Karnams are Niyogi Brahmans who, by custom, have taken up secular jobs. As in most of the surrounding villages, the local Karnams are hereditary patwaris, or village land and revenue officers.

Two other castes have religious functions in Konduru, but their claims to Brahman status are not locally acknowledged. Tambalas light lamps in the Lamp Worship ceremonies of the Shiva temple and make flower garlands for high-caste marriages. Nambis light lamps at the Hanuman shrine. During the month of Kartika, when Hanuman is revered for thirty consecutive nights, an aged Nambi passes through Konduru each evening calling the people to worship.

Aside from visitors there are no Kshatriya or warrior castes represented on the plateau. Vaishyas, however, are present in the Komati caste. Komatis by tradition are moneylenders, bankers, and shopkeepers. Men of other castes have shops and lend money, but the Komati, or Merchants, dominate both trade and finance on the plateau.

There are two kinds of Komati, the Jumpers and the Didn't Jumpers. The distinction is explained in the Shri Vāsavikanyaka Purāna, the sacred scriptures of the Jumpers. According to this history, when the

Merchants first lived in the southern Indian town of Penukunda, the king of the land, while touring the countryside, saw a beautiful Merchant girl named Vāsavikanyaka and demanded that she be prepared for marriage to him upon his return. Facing the disgrace of marrying a man of another caste, even though he was a king from a higher caste, the girl chose to commit suicide by jumping into a fiery pit. She was joined in this act by her father and the heads of one hundred two of the seven hundred fourteen Merchant *gōtras*. Before she jumped to her death the virgin ordered that preference be given to cross-cousin marriages and placed a curse upon all Merchant women that, henceforth, none would be born beautiful. To this day the men declare that no Merchant woman is ever beautiful. Vāsavikanyaka became the patron goddess of the Yegina Komati or Jumpers, those belonging to the *gōtras* whose leaders joined in the mass immolation. They refuse now to associate with the Yegani Komati, the Didn't Jumpers. Each of the one hundred two Yegina *gōtras* has certain foods its members are forbidden to eat.

The Komati illustrate a pattern observed for a number of larger Konduru castes, namely, that the large caste is often surrounded by a number of dependent satellite castes. The Mailalu are beggar priests who visit Konduru periodically bringing images of the Merchant caste deity. The traveling Viramushti entertain the Merchants and the Pagateshagandlu beg at their doors. One sect of Brahmans, serving as gurus for the Merchant caste, expounds caste customs and judges caste disputes.

Like the Brahmans, the Merchants observe the rite of *upanāyana*, the second birth, wherein a boy dons the sacred thread (*janjam*) and becomes a full member of the caste. Castes which practice this rite are often referred to as the twice-born.

The Panchala or artisan castes occupy an unusual place in Konduru. They claim to be Vishva Brahmans, descendants of the five Brahman sages who sprang from the five faces of Vishva Karma, architect of the universe. They wear the *janjam*, or sacred thread of second birth, and refuse to eat food obtained from any other castes, even Brahmans. However, other villagers deny their high rank. Brahmans refuse to officiate at Panchala rites and high castes refuse their food. Old men of the village claim that during their own youth no Hindu castes, not even the untouchables, ate foods prepared by the Panchala.

By trade the Panchala are Craftsmen in gold, iron, wood, brass, and stone. These work monopolies are not, however, strictly enforced. Since there is a shortage of Carpenters in Konduru, the Ironsmiths work both with iron and wood. Interestingly enough, while they are called Ironsmiths in the village, they claim to be descended from the Goldsmith division of the original Panchala. The Konduru Goldsmiths, on the other hand, trace their descent back to the original Ironsmith division. In village life, occupations are important, and caste names are assigned according to vocations practiced. Among the Panchala themselves, however, the original hereditary divisions are still significant.

Below these first three varna, referred to as the twice-born, are a great many castes casually spoken of as Shudras. While they do not wear the sacred thread and, hence, are not the most pure, Shudras do live among the higher castes. By contrast the untouchables of the village live apart and do not associate freely with the varna castemen.

Highest among the Shudras of the plateau are three farming castes: the Velama, the Reddis, and the Kama Kapu. As noted earlier, Velama zamindars ruled the villages of the plateau and surrounding plains during the mid-nineteenth century. Today there are few within the region, but numerous tales persist concerning their once heavy-handed rule. Reddis are the dominant farming caste on the plains to the north and in a number of hamlets on the plateau. Kama Kapus are strong to the southeast, beyond the Krishna River, and a few reside on the eastern edge of the plateau. They are frequent rivals of the Reddis. These three castes together with four smaller Kapu castes trace their mythical origins back to the seven sons of Adi Reddi, a term which might be loosely translated as First Farmer.

The Balija caste cluster includes the Munnur and the Maden, which are both farming castes. The origin of the Munnur (Telugu for three hundred) is associated with several legends. One legend tells of a Kapu woman who gave birth to a son while she was confined in a dungeon with three hundred male prisoners. Not being able to point out the father, she named him Munnur, born of three hundred. According to another legend, King Bhatrahari had three hundred wives from different castes, and their offspring became known as the Munnur.

The Konduru Munnurs claim that once the Madens were also Munnurs. When some Munnurs decided to raise their caste status by prohibiting remarriage of widows and observing Brahmanic rites and others refused to go along with the changes, a split occurred. Now there is no intermarriage between them. Local folk in jest refer to the two castes as the Fruitful (*panta*) caste and the Manure Heap (*penta*) caste. Through the practice of remarriage of widows, the Munnurs are growing in numbers; hence, they are called the Fruitful caste. Maden widows, denied the right of remarriage, have a reputation for being adulterous. The name Manure Heap developed from the local gossip about their burying the refuse of induced abortions in manure piles.

The Braceletmakers and the Pusali castes also belong to the Balija cluster. In the past the Braceletmakers handcrafted the armlets or bangles worn by most village women. With the introduction of factory-made glass bangles, their trade has dwindled. Some have taken up selling the glass bangles from door to door. The Pusali also serve as traveling salesmen, going from house to house selling silver ornaments, necklaces, bracelets, and rings. One endogamous subcaste among them carries the merchandise in a pack on a horse; a second one has established shops in larger villages.

Fruitgatherers are Shudra farmers who have the right to pick forest produce, such as limes, tamarinds, and berries, and to sell them in the marketplace. They also serve as cooks for other Shudras at important festivals.

Some Shudra castes have craft specialties. Fine Weavers prepare cloth from thread brought by a client, and Tailors make cloth into clothes. Today both castes find their vocations threatened by new technologies. Factory-woven cloth commands prestige, and the sewing machine is now used by all castes. To fight these intrusions the Weavers on the plateau have organized a caste union to produce and market their handloomed cloth.

Potters make simple black- and red-ware pots, for only the wealthy can afford silver and brass utensils. Although cheap aluminum ware is now monopolizing the market, potters continue to make the ritual pots needed at marriages and funerals as well as some pots for home use. Potters claim descent from King Shālivāhana and a Kumbhar mother, but other castes ascribe to them a mixed Brahman-Vaishya ancestry.

The Guards and the Bards formerly served in the courts of zamindars and kings, the former as bodyguards and peons, the latter as court musicians and singers. Bards claim that their ancestors were Brahmans in the Kākatīya court of Pratāparudra. According to them this great king raised some fugitive Velama Shudras to high command in his army and sought Brahmans to marry Shudras to Kshatriya women, in hopes of validating the Shudras' claims to warrior status. Most of the Brahmans refused to be accomplices in this tampering with the caste order. A few agreed for a price, but they were later ostracized by the orthodox Brahmans and became known as the Bards. Both the Guards and the Bards have now taken up other vocations. One Guard family in Konduru has the right to repair the village tank dams. The local Bards sell cloth to the poor on credit and then collect payments at harvesttime. They extend credit to people whom the Merchants consider poor risks. Occasionally Bard women still sing at high-caste weddings.

Fishermen fish in the surrounding tanks and streams using casting or drawing nets. They despise the dragline nets used by the Gypsies which are thought to bring bad luck. During the dry season they contract with the village officials for the fishing rights in nearby tanks. When these are almost dried up, they wade out in large groups to catch the fish. Some are sold fresh, but most of the fish are dried and taken to the markets.

Courtesans served formerly as temple entertainers. A distinction should be made between the members of the caste and the dancing girls (*dēva dāsi*) known by the same name. The dancing girls, recruited in the past from many castes and married to the temple deity, were trained in the arts of song, dance, and love. They were accompanied by three men of the Courtesan caste who sang and played instruments while older women joined in, clapping cymbals and singing songs to the amorous Krishna. Such girls offered their services to devotees, and wealthy patrons who paid the costs of their marriage to the deity often claimed first favors. Villagers make a sharp distinction between the favors of the Courtesans and prostitution. The former had a great deal of respectability, and offspring of Courtesan women were considered legitimate. The *dēva dāsis* themselves were thought to bring good fortune. Since they had been married to the gods, they could never become widows who were thought to bring bad luck. Even now they are asked to lead marriage and religious processions for this reason. Their property seems to have been inherited by their real or adopted daughters. Sons could claim only maintenance and marriage costs.

Regarding the Courtesan caste, Hassan states (1920:95): "The sons of dancing girls and such of their daughters as are too plain to take to prostitution have formed a separate caste of their own, governed by the same laws of matrimony and inheritance as are prevalent among other Telugu castes." There are several such castes; some are Hindu and some Muslim. The former belong to a cluster of castes called the Telaga. Castes in this cluster were formed from offspring of mixed marriages; chiefly they were the illegitimate offspring of high Shudra women by men of higher castes. Several Courtesan families live in Konduru. They claim to have given up their caste profession; however, several of the older women were married to the gods in their youth and had sons by unknown fathers.

Herdsmen are a large pastoral caste in Telingana. They maintain large herds of cattle and flocks of sheep of their own, or they contract to herd animals for others. Konduru Herdsmen move with their animals into the forests during the dry season. One brother or partner may take his turn in herding the animals while another is at home gathering supplies. Some reportedly have two wives; one wife maintains the village home and the other one the camp. Herdsmen have at least eighteen endogamous subcastes (four of which are resident on the plateau) as well as totemic exogamous *gōtras*. The Paita *gōtra*, for instance, will not eat the Paita vegetables; the Komirilu do not use *komirilu* or double poles in constructing their houses; and the Sheshala do not throw rice for good luck upon newlyweds at their marriage.

The Kuruva, also a pastoral caste, are noted for weaving prized goat-hair blankets which are used as cloaks in cold weather, as raincoats during the rains, and as covers at night. Some five generations back, during the era of the zamindars, Kanarese-speaking Kuruvas from beyond Bider came to the plateau and settled at Rameshvaram and Tartikol. Over the years they have used what turned into a "corrupt form" or dialect of Kanarese at home (Telugu is used at the marketplace), but have lost most of their contacts with Kuruvas elsewhere. They have now formed an endogamous enclave of about three hundred households on the plateau.

Winetappers formerly had a monopoly for the extraction of palm sap from the trees growing alongside the streams. This sap ferments overnight and is sold the next day at the beer parlors on the edge of the village. In recent decades the government changed from its collection of a fixed tax per tree to contracting a given territory to the highest bidder. This procedure opened the way for others to participate in the lucrative trade. In some areas, the Winetappers have organized into caste unions which hold the contracts; however, the Konduru Winetappers lack the unity and resources to do so. Their lament is that each family should share in the rights, but no one wants to contribute to a common fund.

Members of the Servant caste formerly served as household workers of petty lords, and members of the Beggar caste lived by entertaining villagers and begging. Now members of both castes work as manual laborers.

At the bottom of the Shudra castes are two large service castes, the Washermen and the Barbers. Washermen wash clothes for all the other castes. Because they handle dirty clothing and cloth defiled by menstruation and childbirth, they rank low. However, they are permitted to live within the respected caste community. Washermen and Potters also serve as priests for the village goddesses. Brahmans never participate in these ceremonies since they require the sacrifice of blood.

Barbers shave the men of Konduru, except for the untouchables who must ask the Barber for the right to use his knife and pay him an annual levy of grain at harvesttime. Barbers are the village surgeons; they lance boils, and pull teeth, just as barbers of an earlier day did in Europe. Their wives often assist in the birth of a child by handling the knife used to sever the umbilical cord. Barbers are also the village musicians.

Hindu varna castes constitute the dominant community in most plateau villages. Within their ranks there are men to perform all the essential crafts and services necessary for maintaining community life — all, that is, except the most defiling jobs. Furthermore, these castes control the village leadership, its economic assets, and its religious orthodoxy.

Harijan Castes

A second community in many plateau villages consists of the ritually polluting castes, variously referred to as untouchables, outcastes, pariahs, and Harijans. In the approved bureaucratic jargon of the Indian government they are called the scheduled castes. Such castes live apart from the main village, for they are considered defiling to the varna castemen. Religiously the Harijans have only a marginal Hindu orientation; while some of their gods are identified with Hindu deities, the Harijans do not enter the Hindu temples of the plateau or have Brahmans as their priests.

The plateau has two prominent Harijan castes, Weavers and Leatherworkers; both consist of a group of subcastes. The main Weaver caste has more than thirty subcastes formed on the basis of such factors as territory, language, religious sect, and specific high-caste origin. Associated with the Weaver caste are such symbiotic castes as the Weaver Priests, Weaver Musicians, and Weaver Acrobats. Most Weavers on the plateau work for wealthy landlords, but many have acquired at least a few acres of land of their own.

Leatherworkers are defiled because they handle dead animals and tan skins. Like the Weavers they form the core for a caste cluster. Baine serve as their priests, Madiga Mashti as their entertainers, and Sindu as their dramatists. Leatherworkers claim that they and the Panchala castes were the original inhabitants of the land. According to a Leatherworker legend, Jambhu, the great rishi, had six sons. These sons shared the rights to weave the sacred thread of the twice-born before it was stolen by the Brahmans. Of these, Leatherworker was the eldest. The others were Ironsmith, Carpenter, Brass-smith, Rocksmith, and Goldsmith. One day as these brothers were preparing a buffalo-meat curry for a feast, a piece of meat fell on the ground. The Leatherworker picked it up, blew it off, and threw it back into the pot. The others were incensed and threw him out of the caste. Despite their debasement the Leatherworkers claim that the five artisan castes still respect them and share ritual ties with them.

Marginal Castes

Certain castes and tribes are marginal to the Indian peasant village: economically they live in a symbiotic relationship with the village; socially they live apart. These groups are of theoretical interest because they are in the process of joining the caste community. Most of them enter as Shudra castes, in the middle of the caste order, rather than as untouchables at the bottom.

The Chenchu tribe is divided into two groups. The Deva Chenchus (God's Chenchus) are a hunting and gathering tribe living in the forests south of Konduru. Roots, berries, and small game are their basis of subsistence; in addition, they gather forest fruits, broom grass, and honey to sell to the local villages. A few hire out as laborers to contractors who exploit such forest produce as bamboo, teak, and leaves for wrapping cigarettes. The meager earnings of the laborers are immediately spent on staples and strong drink. During the dry season when food is scarce the Chenchus subsist largely on the flowers of the *ippa* tree, which they grind into a mush or brew into a high-protein beer — mainly they choose to do the latter. The cool evenings are spent dancing, drinking, and singing but they often end in brawls. Government attempts to settle the Chenchus in the forest and to teach them agriculture have had only moderate success.

The Village Chenchus claim to be a branch of the forest tribe which had settled near the plateau villages. They construct huts similar to those of their forest counterparts and share common names and a dialect. They assert that an exchange of brides with the forest folk is possible but that their girls are not prepared for the dangers of a forest life. The Forest Chenchus, in turn, consider themselves superior to the Village Chenchus.

Another marginal caste is the Lambardi, a colorful gypsy people who live apart in separate hamlets called *tandas*, speak their own language, and maintain unique cultural patterns. Before the introduction of roads and railroads the Gypsies were a caste of transporters, carrying merchandise from town to town by large caravans of pack animals. Some took exports to coastal cities and returned with salt to sell in the interior. During times of war they were hired by military commanders to forage for the army and its mounts — a task which gave them the reputation of being thieves. Today, under government persuasion, the plateau Gypsies have taken up agriculture and cattle herding.

TRANSIENT CASTES

Around both clean and polluting sedentary castes are clustered a great number of transient castes whose members constantly visit the villages. These include entertainers, historians, bards, priests, magicians, soothsayers, mendicants, and herbal doctors. Some are suppliers of baskets, others of woven oxcart covers, and still others of palm-leaf mats. There are vendors of fine cloth, coarse cloth, jewelry, blankets, pots and pans, and sacred books. There are traveling Brahmans who solicit funds from higher castes for publication of their ancient caste histories and rites, and beggars who wander with either bells, gourd instruments, cymbals, horns, harmoniums, or any one of a variety of different drums. Some entertainers appear with bears, monkeys, or cobras and mongooses, while others come with costumes and dramas or leather puppets. Others are acrobats, jugglers, tumblers, or singers. Mendicants come with sacred cows, sacred stories, sacred images, sacred herbs, or yellow robes and beggar's bowls.

Most transient castes are Hindus. Members of some transient castes serve as priests, gurus, historians, or beggars for the members of a single sedentary caste. Some call only at varna caste homes, others at untouchable homes, and still others go to homes of any caste. Many of them divide the territory with their fellow castemen and travel around a regular circuit. Thirty-eight different wandering castes (see Appendix I) were represented in the transient groups that came to Konduru village during the year and a half of this study. Naturally, this list does not include all those who might appear over a longer span of time, or those who might have been overlooked during this period.

Still other castes might be classified as semitribal transients. They are migratory workers who stay in an area as long as they can earn a living, and then move on. They live in bands and camp in the fields. Quarrymen extract rock from the surrounding hills for buildings and grindstones. Earthmovers dig wells, build earthen dams, and construct roads. Rockcrushers crush rock for use in surfacing roads. Soothsayers read palms, tell fortunes, hunt birds and small game, weave baskets, and herd pigs. They also speak an exotic language that is not understood by others. All of these transient groups are only loosely integrated with the village and its Hindu traditions.

MUSLIM CASTES

Over the centuries Muslims in Konduru have adapted the concepts of caste to their own community. In theory they do not fit into the caste structure, which Muslims themselves often admit. But Muslims are members of the village and thus must be integrated into village life if there is to be stability.

Several factors have influenced the rank of Muslims on the plateau. Because they do not proscribe eating meat, marrying widows, or the taking of life, they should be ranked, in theory, below the varna castes. Yet until 1949, Muslims ruled Hyderabad State in which Konduru was located, and local Muslims held many of the offices that commanded power and respect. Only since independence has the Muslim community assumed its present status which is on the level of the low Shudras.

In accordance with their religious teachings, the Muslims state that they eat with anyone. In marriage, however, they have endogamous castes. The highest rank goes to the "Arabs," who claim direct ancestry from the land of Mohammed. Under the Nizams, a few Arabs served in the government offices of Konduru; now only a single aged Arab lives there.

The Turks are the largest of the Muslim castes on the plateau. The name probably has reference to the fact that during the rule of the Nizams numerous free lancers came to Hyderabad from Persia and Turkey. Konduru Turks speak of four subcastes: Sayeds, Sheikhs, Mogals, and Patans; however, only the first three are present in Konduru. The Sayeds claim descent from the Prophet and refuse to intermarry with the others. From their ranks come the local religious leaders.

There are other Muslim castes. Fakirs are traveling mendicants, entertainers, and beggars. Kartikes are the village butchers. Before killing a sheep or goat, they perform *hallāl* and ritually ask the pardon of the animal to be slain. Such meat is considered free from defilement and is eaten by the higher Shudras as well as by the Muslims. All of these Muslim castes speak Urdu in their homes, and, when able, isolate their women in *pūrdah.* By contrast, the low-ranking Cottoncarders speak Telugu in the home and used to employ their women to card the cotton brought to them by the villagers.

The Muslim castes of Konduru live with the Hindu varna castes in the central village. Many of them have taken new jobs opened by recent changes. They manage the tea stalls and one of the restaurants in Konduru, drive the trucks exporting produce, and operate many of the sewing machines found in the marketplace.

The extent to which caste has segmented Indian society is hard to imagine. Within any region there are many dozen castes, each claiming to have cultural distinctions of its own. It is impossible to trace the boundaries of each such caste over space and time since the culture is neither static nor homogeneous. New castes are being formed by territorial division, migration, fission of existent castes, conversion to new sects, occupational association, miscegenation, assimilation of tribes, or historical accident. Others are dying out or merging. Some castes rise in position through the exploitation of their resources and power; others lose out through unfortunate circumstances in the flowing dynamics of rivalry and alliance. Changes in one area frequently do not occur in other areas because of the fragmentation of castes into local groups and the lack of communication between these groups.

The caste structure is not simply an aggregate of culturally distinct groups; it is a system. Under careful observation, what at first appears to be a patchwork quilt turns out to be a mosaic. Castes and subcastes are linked together by networks of interdependence. It is this system of caste groups, rather than castes as societal categories, that provides the village with its stability.

CHAPTER THREE

SOCIAL GROUPS

CASTE and varna have captured the imagination of observers because they portray, in a form unparalleled elsewhere, the application of certain structural principles carried to their logical limits. But while societal categories provide the mental frameworks for life, social groups translate it into action. In operation, castes are broken up into local groups which are the basis for social interaction on the level of the village. Caste groups are not the only ones of significance in the village; the range is wide and varied. The observations on social groups made here apply primarily to the sedentary communities of Konduru, which often differ markedly from transient bands and tribes.

THE FAMILY

The family pattern most evident in Konduru is the lineal family which "links families of procreation of several married siblings to their parents" (Murdock 1965:181). The ideal family, according to the villagers, is the extended family, but even they admit that most families break up within two or three years after the death of both parents. In my own observations, lineal families, with an occasional exception, broke up within a few months after the death of the patriarch. Men blame their wives for the splits, but rivalries and inheritance disputes often breed enmity between brothers themselves. As one informant stated, alluding to the great war between lineage brothers in the epic Mahabharata, "There are Pandavas and Kauravas in every family."

In lineal families, married sons construct huts for their families against the larger house. Quarrels within the family frequently result in separate cooking arrangements within the larger household. Occasionally, when parents are old and the arguments severe, the brothers part company; parents and unmarried siblings then become the responsibility of the eldest son who also receives a larger share of the inheritance.

Membership in the lineal family may be clearly defined, but the members present in the household at any given time vary considerably. Brides are brought in and daughters are married out — these transitions, though, are gradual. Since marriage often takes place before the bride reaches puberty, after the ceremony she returns to her parents' home. Only upon receiving formal word of her first menses does the husband go with suitable gifts for his parents-in-law to bring his wife home. Even then, on important festive occasions, a wife visits her parents for extended periods of time. Later, during the fifth or seventh month of her first pregnancy, the young wife goes to her mother's home for the delivery and then returns home in an odd-numbered month (even numbers are considered unlucky). After each visit, the husband or his stand-in must escort her back home. A wife frequently spends a quarter or more of her early married life in the home of her youth. As a wife develops roles and responsibilities in her husband's home, she spends more and more time there. Visits to her parents become shorter and less frequent and, in the end, she finds her primary loyalties are to her husband and children.

Resident males are also absent from the home for extended periods of time. Before the harvest farmers have to guard their crops from birds and thieves in the day and wild pigs from the nearby forest at night. Pastoralists accompany their herds deep into the forest for weeks, while wage earners and laborers leave their families at home when they are away on distant jobs. As a result the responsibilities for maintaining the home and preparing the meals for resident family members fall to the women, and, in particular, to the wife of the patriarch or the wife of the eldest son.

The day-to-day composition of the household is changed by extended visits from relatives in need or on business trips and by fellow castemen stopping for a night's lodging. The fluid nature of the household is accentuated by divorce. High castes prohibit divorce and punish the violators, but divorce is practiced by many Shudras, Muslims, and Harijans. As will be evident later, many village councils are called to disentangle the problems of marriage.

Village elders justify the transient nature of the family by appealing to the four stages of life prescribed by Hinduism: student, householder, hermit, and mendicant. As Goldsmith Lakshayya, the village philosopher, noted, "In his old age a man ought to turn his affairs over to his sons and give the last years of his life to God." Villagers respect the few aged men of Konduru who have given themselves to spiritual meditations in their homes, but they are skeptical of the ocher-robed mendicants (*sannyāsins*) who beg for a livelihood. Nor is their skepticism unfounded, for mendicancy not only serves religious purposes, it also acts as a safety valve providing an avenue of escape for men caught in a social bind. A man who abandons his family is condemned, but a man who leaves it to worship God is honored.

The contrast of motives can be seen in those of two local men who donned ocher robes. The first, a Brahman accountant, turned his rights over to his brother in 1964 and set up camp in an abandoned temple in the hopes of gaining spiritual merit by reviving the worship there. The other, a merchant, left his wife because of family strife and went on a three-year pilgrimage to northern Indian shrines. Only after his wife left for her own village did he return to set up shop again in Konduru.

Land and work rights belong to all male members of the family and cannot be alienated without the consent of the grown sons. When a man leaves his village, he does not immediately lose his rights. For a time he may delegate them to another, but in the long run, they must be activated to be recognized. Rights not exercised for two or three generations cannot be claimed, even if remembered.

Women also claim rights in their natal homes. Their support until marriage and the wedding costs are supposed to be borne by their families. Parents or brothers are also expected to give a married woman gifts of clothing at least once a year during her visits; furthermore, a pot of grain from each harvest belongs to her. If a woman should be abandoned by her husband or widowed, she may return with her children to live in her parents' home.

Parents with no male heir seek an adoptive marriage (*ilitum*) in which the bride stays in her natal family, and a husband willing to assume the responsibilities of a son is adopted. The children take lineage affiliation through their mother. In a culture in which jural recognition is given to patrilineal descent, the fiction of adoption is used to justify the transfer of rights and descent through a daughter. Men look upon entering an *ilitum* marriage as a sign of losing some respect — only those with poor prospects at home agree to it. Out of two hundred seven marriages recorded in Konduru in 1965, ten were *ilitum.*

In the absence of any offspring, parents may adopt a child; often the male child of the husband's brother is chosen. This child loses all rights in the home of his birth and gains those of the home of his filiation. Should later children enter such a home by birth, the filiated son theoretically retains the rights of a full son. In one observed case, however, the sons by descent attempted to exclude the adopted son from his share of the patrimony. Only when he appealed to the village elders was he given a small share.

THE LOCAL PATRILINEAGE

A second group of importance to the individual is made up of the local members of one's patrilineage. This group plays a major role in caste and personal rituals. No other ceremony reveals the importance of the patrilineage as clearly as does the marriage rite. From the earliest negotiations to the successful tying of the wedding cord, marriage ceremonies are carried out as the activity of two kin groups. Gift exchanges and formal receptions for the representatives of each family accompany every step in the elaborate rituals.

In the Edurukolu ceremony preceding a high-caste marriage, the two kin groups are formally introduced to each other. Watchmen stationed at the edge of the village herald the arrival of the groom's party on the night the wedding ceremonies begin. Men from the bride's party escort them to the meeting place in a street or courtyard where the groom is seated on a mat of honor surrounded by his kinsmen (there are minor variations if the ceremonies take place at the groom's village). The bride is brought and seated on another mat a dozen yards away accompanied by her relatives. While chanting the proper mantras and performing suitable rites the Brahman priest introduces the bride's parents to the groom, whereupon they give the groom gifts of clothing and ceremonially wash his feet to show their respect. Similarly the groom's parents are taken to meet the bride and to give gifts

Fisherman at work in the nearby reservoir

Washermen at work. A washerman is beating the clothes on a rock to clean them while the wife is soaking the other clothes nearby

Putting the steel rim on the oxcart wheel

Procession of Rama and Sita on the temple chariot (or car)

Transient entertainers with their trained bears

The Homan (five) ceremonies during the Konduru jatva celebrating the marriage of Rama and Sita

Temple Priest performing the annual marriage of Rama and Sita

of clothing to her. Women from each group place red spots on the foreheads of the women of the other group, and boys pass among the opposite parties dabbing wrists with perfume and sprinkling scented water. In a grand finale, everyone throws a pinch or two of white ash upon the members of the other party as a sign of goodwill, and all retire to the bride's home for a welcome feast.

The marriage ceremony itself involves both kin groups in prescribed rites marking the changes in status of the new couple. The bride is entrusted by her kin to the groom's relatives, who in turn pledge to safeguard her health and welfare. In the end gifts are given to the couple — to the groom by his relatives and to the bride by hers. All watch excitedly as a secretary duly records each gift, giver, and recipient, for the relatives of the winner take pride in their generosity. Wedding gifts constitute part of the web of obligations binding lineages together. At successive marriages in the lineage, previous gifts are remembered and comparable ones are expected in return.

Lineage groups safeguard the rights of their respective members during married life, particularly when the partners come from different villages. Relatives of the bride given to a distant village have no voice in the caste council that settles disputes there. Their only recourse is either to bring pressure to bear upon the caste elders of that village or to bring their daughter back home.

A man also has close ties to his wife's kin. They may care for his family when he is away at some distant job. They can also help him find a suitable daughter-in-law when he arranges the marriage of his son. Not all women of his caste are suitable brides. Within each caste there are those who are *kaltri* (the Urdu form is *biriki*) or of doubtful ancestry. The best guarantee of securing a girl who is not of mixed-caste ancestry is to select one from the lineage from which the father himself obtained his wife.

A man, in search of a bride for his son, may ask his wife's brother for his daughter. Such matrilateral cross-cousin marriages are referred to as *manirkam*. In all Konduru's Hindu castes except for two of the Brahman castes, *manirkam* is the preferred form of marriage. Merchants say that in their caste a young man may demand the hand of his unwed cross-cousin and, in one case that I observed, a wealthy Merchant uncle bought off a poor nephew whom he did not want as a son-in-law. Strangely enough, the Merchants of Konduru show the lowest incidence of cross-cousin marriage of the castes tabulated (see Table 2).

Two other special forms of marriage are recognized: marriage to one's sister's daughter and patrilateral cross-cousin marriage (marriage to a father's sister's daughter); neither of these is common. According to villagers, a man must respect his father's sister and her children. If he marries one of her daughters, he is in no position to discipline his wife. A mother's brother, on the other hand, is expected to respect his sister's son and support him when he quarrels with his wife.

Table 2. Frequency of Marriages for each Caste according to Type and Residence

Caste	Brahman	Merchant	Goldsmith	Tailor	Mummur	Washerman	Barber
Number of marriages examined	22	31	16	4	22	84	78
Type of marriage							
Percentage mother's brother's daughter ..	13.6	6.5	25.0	25.0	32.0	20.0	14.0
Percentage sister's daughter	0	0	0	25.0	4.5	1.0	3.8
Percentage plural ...	9.1	0	0	0	13.6	2.4	3.8
Residence							
Percentage of patrilocal	84.2	83.9	81.0	75.0	83.3	90.4	93.3
Percentage of matrilocal	0	6.4	0	0	5.6	7.2	4.0
Percentage neolocal .	15.8	9.7	19.0	25.0	11.1	2.4	2.7

Lacking marriageable girls among his wife's kinfolk, a father can explore the chain of reference from one trusted kin group to the next (*silisila*). Accompanied by his brother-in-law, a man can visit the relatives of his brother-in-law's wife in search of a bride. Though these two parties may never have met, they can trust one another for they are linked by marriage ties to the same man. If these people have no daughter to offer, they can escort him to still other lineage groups in the marriage chain, or vouch for him to their fellow villagers.

Multiple marriage ties linking villages also engender confidence between patrilineages. Konduru Washermen are linked by single marriage ties to only five villages beyond Achampet; this accounts for twelve percent of the Washermen marriages examined (see Table 3). They are linked by two marriage ties to six villages, forming a total of twenty-eight percent of the marriages. Sixty percent of their marriages are with communities where there are three or more marriage ties. Similarly, Leatherworkers of one plains village are linked to Konduru by eight marriage ties, involving fifty-four percent of all the Konduru Leatherworkers who married people off the plateau.

Table 3. Frequency Distribution of Marriage Ties between Different Castes in Konduru and Those in Villages beyond Achampet

Villages Linked to Konduru by Marriage	Washerman	Barber	Leatherworker
Linked by only one marriage			
Number of villages	5	8	5
Number of marriages...................	5	8	5
Percentage of marriages................	12	21	33
Linked by two marriages			
Number of villages....................	6	10	1
Number of marriages..................	12	20	2
Percentage of marriages................	28	53	13
Linked by three or more marriages			
Number of villages....................	6	2	1
Number of marriages..................	26	10	8
Percentage of marriages................	60	26	54

A father seeking a husband for his daughter must consider other factors. It is difficult to visit, and, if need be, defend a daughter who lives far away. For Konduru, the average radius of marriages for the most populous castes such as the Weavers and Leatherworkers is less than ten miles (see Table 4). For smaller castes the radius increases. The combined influence of territory and chains of reference upon the selection of brides is evident from the following facts: while in 1936 there were 269,492 Washermen in Telengana alone (one of three Telugu-speaking regions, Husain 1939:50), thirty-one percent of the Washermen marriages involving Konduru were between inhabitants of three villages on the plateau, and eighty-eight percent of the marriages involved multiple ties.

Finally, it is the patrilineage relatives that grieve for one's death. Lineal relatives of the deceased are considered ritually polluted, generally for ten days. Members of the immediate family may observe mourning rites for longer periods of time; this can extend for up to a

Table 4. Origin of Marriage Partners by Territory and Caste (measured in percent)

Caste	Number of Marriages Examined	Konduru Village and Hamlets	Plateau	Achampet Taluk	Nagarkurnool, Kalvakurthi and Deverakonda Taluks	Beyond	Mean Radius of Marriage in Miles
Brahman	22	0	0	13.6	54.5	31.9	103
Merchant	31	9	34	21	27	9	35
Goldsmith	16	0	21	50	29	0	20
Munnur	22	0	0	0	95.5	4.5	42
Tailor	4	0	25	0	75	0	43
Washerman	84	6	25	48.8	20.2	0	20
Barber	78	9.3	17.3	18.6	48.1	6.7	36
Weaver	53	10	78	12	0	0	6
Leatherworker	40	28.5	33	38.5	0	0	7

year among the Merchants for the death of an aged patriarch. On the eleventh day, the kinsmen gather for purification. They bathe and wash their clothes, and the men have their heads shaved. A priest performs the necessary rites and places a new mark on each man's head. Then all gather for a fellowship meal.

The local patrilineal group provides an individual with his closest associates and his chief social support. Linked together by chains of marriage, patrilineal groups constitute in their widest range the endogamous subcaste.

THE CASTE GROUP

More inclusive and more significant in terms of group interaction on the village level are the local caste groups, each of which is composed of people in the village belonging to a single caste. Fellow castemen are important in family rituals such as marriage. At least one representative from each local caste home should be present; failure to send an invitation to each home is enough to disrupt a wedding. Similarly, local castemen gather to mourn the death of one of their group. But caste groups function primarily to regulate caste affairs and to protect the interests of its members in the village. Those groups which are small or disorganized frequently lose out in the power struggles of the village, as can be seen in a case which took place in Konduru in 1963.

ᏬᏬThe Konduru Weavers used to pay the Barbers an annual sum of grain for the use of their knives, but like other Harijans they had to shave themselves. After a young Weaver learned barbering in a large town and began shaving the Weavers for a few pennies, the Barbers raised a furor. The Weavers informed the Barbers that they could keep their work rights if they came personally and shaved the Harijans. The high castes heard that the Barbers were seriously considering shaving the Harijans and they too sent word; they would refuse to give their business to any one who shaved the untouchables. Caught between the two alternatives and lacking the unity or power to enforce their rights over the Weavers, the Barbers remained quiet. Now the Weavers have their own barber.ᏬᏬ

Local castemen must also protect their interests against men of their own caste from other regions, who come and do not respect the local caste authorities. In 1964, an incident occurred when a Washerman from a distant village interfered with local Washerman politics.

ↄↄThe men of Madenvanpalli quarrelled with their household Washermen and, in a fit of rage, fired them all. The villagers then called in a Washerman from a distant village and gave him the laundry rights in their hamlet. When the local Washermen heard this, they met and mapped out their strategy. First the Washermen elders confronted the intruder and offered him two hundred rupees to leave. When he refused, a band of youths waylaid him one night. The man understood the message and left the next day. A few Washermen spent two weeks in the local jail, but their work monopolies had been preserved.ↄↄ

Caste groups guard the privileges of a caste in the village. They enforce caste customs and organize efforts to raise the caste status by prohibiting such practices as the eating of meat or the remarrying of widows. They arrange for the construction of caste shrines and propitiate the gods by organizing festivals and temple worship. Finally, as will be seen later, caste groups play an important role in the settlement of disputes within the village.

ASSOCIATIONS

Preoccupation with caste has led, for the most part, to a neglect of the importance of associations within the Indian village. Associations are both common and varied, and by cutting across caste barriers they help to integrate the village.

A common type of social interaction is the *bajana,* a songfest in which men gather for a night of religious singing. Occasional sessions are arranged by a host who invites his friends, prepares a small shrine, and provides items needed in the service such as coconuts, incense, colored powder, sugar, oil, and lights. After the devotees have gathered, a choirmaster leads them in some preliminary hymns. Then he begins the sacred ballad, which will be continued throughout the night. He sings a line; the guests repeat it while clapping their hands to the rhythm. He continues, line by line, narrating the stories of the god. Songs begin softly and slowly. Gradually the tension mounts, the tempo quickens, voices rise, and heads bend back in ecstasy. The trance is broken in a climax of chanting, clapping, and shouts of victory. Incense and coconuts are offered to the god. There is some casual conversation and an inspired worshiper sings a solo or leads the group in a devotional song. Then the leader resumes the narrative. During the evening the priest comes to lead the party in the formal worship rituals.

Some *bajana* associations are more permanent. Groups of young men who sing together often form informal *bajana* choirs which are invited to lead larger services in the homes of the rich. There are also temple *bajana* associations in which male devotees gather weekly in the temple to sing. During 1965 Konduru had two such temple associations: one in the Rama temple sponsored regularly by the progressive young men of town and the other in the Shiva temple sporadically revived by their rivals, a clique of orthodox Merchants.

Just as does singing, drama offers an occasion for young men to form associations. Movies based on the religious stories of India have become a major form of entertainment in many villages, and Konduru villagers who can afford to do so visit Achampet, the nearest town having electricity and a theater. But of more importance to the plateau villagers are the many indigenous forms of drama which have been part of their heritage for generations. Many of these dramas are staged by specific caste groups. Men of the Leather-puppeteer caste tour villages putting on shadow plays using colorful translucent leather puppets behind white sheets. Beggars and bards of many castes stage street productions to attract generous audiences. Some use elaborate costumes, others bring brass figures or hand puppets. Some sing in the streets during the day, and some perform in the village square at night. Some castes perform only for select audiences: the Viramushti for their patrons, the Merchants; Puja Pagateshagandlu for Brahmans and Farmers; Podapatras for Herdsmen; Adep Sings for Barbers; and Mashtis for Harijans. In addition, professional troupes stage elaborate productions of classic dramas in temporary shelters and charge admission fees.

For local entertainment, drama associations composed of young men perform *burakathas*, *harikathas* (ballads), *bhāgya nātakams* (semi-classical dramas), and *vīdi nātakams* (street dramas). A brief description will illustrate the general characteristics of these types of groups. Young men organize a street drama association and arrange for a guru to teach them the songs. After practice has continued at night for several months and elaborate costumes are prepared, they seek out a wealthy patron who is willing to pay twenty or thirty rupees for a performance. In return, the patron is publicly honored during the event as the sponsor

of free entertainment for the villagers. A crier announces the performance through the streets; a dressing room is constructed at one end of the
village square with bamboo poles and blankets, and gas lights are hung
from nearby posts. Families arrive with their children and squat on the
ground or catch quick naps on their mats. All are ready around nine
o'clock.

The performance begins with music — a chorus accompanied by
drums and a few assorted instruments. One by one, each character
dresses in the cubicle; then he bursts from behind the curtain to the
cheers of the chorus. The first is a king, but which king? He drops a
hint here, a clue there, as the audience tries to guess his identity. A
clown enters, ridiculing the king and uttering asides to the audience
about some shady sides of the king's past life. Someone in the audience shouts a jibe at the king and the others laugh. No one loses the
thread of the story in the confusion. Each line is sung and resung by
the leader. Each line is echoed and reechoed by the chorus. A half
hour passes, but only the first character has been introduced.

The second character appears, a young man dressed as a queen.
The queen dominates the scene for a quarter of an hour during which
time the clown drops by to make passes at her. By two or three in
the morning all the characters have been introduced and the plot
thickens. Those who have stretched out to sleep are awakened and
kept informed by others. Kings and tyrants march back and forth
across the stage. Right is about to triumph when suddenly the tyrant's
aide turns out to be a demon who overpowers the hero. Now that all
seems lost, the hero's charioteer reveals himself to be a god in disguise.
The battle which began between men becomes a cosmic struggle between all the forces of good and evil, but right triumphs in the end.
Dawn is breaking when the last blows are struck and gods, demons,
kings, and queens march off the stage to trek around the village and
collect a few gifts of grain or coins.

Village bands are another type of association. Leatherworkers have
the right to beat the large leather drums, and other castes claim certain other instruments, but Barbers have the right to organize and
play in the regular village bands. Old men still form the traditional
type of band using the *suti* (flute), *shehnai* (indigenous oboe), *tālam*
(cymbals), and *dōlu* (a type of drum). Younger Barbers with government aid have formed two modern style bands in Konduru which com-

pete for the opportunities to perform at weddings and festivals. Elaborate weddings will have two or three such bands playing popular tunes heard over the radio.

In the economic sphere, women's work groups transplant rice and harvest crops. Those belonging to such groups obtain work more consistently than women without such affiliation. Farmers contact group leaders who call the women to work, supervise the task, and distribute the total earnings. These leaders keep a slightly larger share of the profits for themselves.

Religious associations of a guru and his disciples form relatively stable groups cutting across religious as well as caste boundaries. These gurus must be distinguished from those belonging to guru castes that have inherited the role of mentor for specific castes. The former attract disciples from all walks of life, Hindu and Muslim, clean and Harijan, who gather for spiritual advice and fellowship. Some have widespread followings and may maintain retreat centers or *āshrams* where their disciples congregate. Others attract only a small following from a few villages, as was the case with Latif Sahib, the Konduru Saint.

᭞᭞Latif Sahib was a Muslim forest ranger who became known around Konduru as a saint. Before his death, in 1958, he had a local following of Hindus and Muslims who came to him for spiritual instruction. Since his death, these disciples have continued to meet annually on the anniversary of his death. After a *bajana* held in one of the homes, they go in a procession at night to the newly whitewashed tomb where cloths are draped over the shrine, food and incense offered, flowers strewn, prayer flags raised, and prayers recited. Hindu devotees crack coconuts and kiss the tomb. Then the disciples continue their song service throughout the night in a nearby shelter. ᭞᭞

COMMUNITIES

Using Olsen's definition (1968:91) of community as a social organization that is "territorially localized and through which its members satisfy most of their daily needs and deal with most of their common problems," one can properly speak of various levels of communities in Konduru. None of these is totally self-sufficient, but each in some measure is self-contained in the range of needs it satisfies and the services it renders. One can refer to the caste group as a community on one level and to the village as a community on another. However, there is a level of community between these which is easily overlooked.

As noted in Chapter Two, the resident castes of Konduru are divided by religion and the concepts of ritual pollution into three intermediate communities: the Hindu varna community, the Harijans, and the Muslims. While it is true that among Hindu varna castes there are different levels of pollution or purity, the difference between the varna castes and the Harijans is of another order. Each of these communities can be differentiated from the others in certain respects, while in other respects they overlap one another. Differences between these communities are most apparent in the areas of religion and entertainment. Each has its own temples, mosques, or shrines; stages its own dramas and *bajanas*; and celebrates its own festivals. Associations, for the most part, are confined to a single community.

The Hindu varna castes observe many of the Brahmanic rites of the Hindu great tradition. Their gods, Rama and Shiva and others, generally are found throughout India. Their temples, reserved for the religiously clean, are the centers of worship in Konduru. Their ceremonies, administered by Brahman priests who incant Sanskrit mantras, follow Puranic tradition. Annually they organize a village fair at the Rama temple, and folk from other villages come to share in the festivity.

Men of the varna castes also unite in the celebration of some of the traditional Hindu festivals. On Ugadi (Telugu New Year) they gather in front of the temple, where the priest reads the horoscopes of the coming year for their crops, their community, and their families. On Dasara men escort the gods to the Jami trees outside the village. Their requests for divine blessing are written on pieces of paper, which are then hidden in the hollows of the trees. Men exchange Jami leaves with each other as a symbol of goodwill, and rivals are pressured to forget their disputes, at least for the day.

Muslims have their own god, mosque, prayer wall, sacred book, festival days, and priests. In the home they observe different rites conducted by their own religious leaders who recite prayers in Arabic. They organize their own entertainment and share a common mythology.

In some respects the Harijans of Konduru are less of a community.

The Weavers have their own temple for Malikarjuna and the Leather-workers have a shrine for Jamavanthudu. Each caste has its own priests and religious fairs. Those converted to Christianity have their own church in a nearby hamlet, their own minister, and their Bible. Harijans do, however, join together in staging performances and cele-brating certain festivals. On occasion they unite in opposing the varna castes — theirs is a unity born out of a common social plight.

Each of these communities shares certain characteristics with an-other to the exclusion of the third. Varna Hindus and most Harijans share in differing degrees in the great Hindu traditions of India. They identify their gods with the Hindu deities, observe some of the same festivals, sing the same songs, and enact the great epics in their dramas. Both use Telugu in the home in contrast to the Muslims, who use Urdu. Both share dress styles; their women wear saris, their men use *panchas* and, occasionally, turbans. Muslim women wear a *kamēz* and *shālwar* or a *burka* and their men wear long coats or plaid *dhotis*. A few village men, usually those in government services, wear Western-style pants and shirts. The essential job monopolies and the full fluo-rescence of caste are found in the Hindu communities. With the excep-tion of the Cottoncarders, who appear to have been Hindu converts to Islam, Muslims have no vital occupational monopolies. Hindu castes, irrespective of community, also have many personal names in common.

Hindu varna and Muslim castes reside in the same territory. While castes tend to congregate along certain streets and lanes, there is no marked segregation between the two religious groups. Harijans, how-ever, live apart from the main village in enclaves or in hamlets a few furlongs away.

Finally, one finds Harijans and Muslims do have some traits in common: both use meat and liquor freely and accept food prepared by the clean castes; both are power minorities due to their large sizes; and both are used as allies by the powerful varna castes.

Hindu varna castes form the core of Konduru. They have status, power, and orthodoxy. Muslims and Harijans form peripheral com-munities outside the formal caste structure. Beyond these are a num-ber of relatively independent marginal communities. The Gypsies of Konduru live apart, speak their own language, stage their own enter-tainment, and worship their own gods. The cultural differences are readily observable in the ornate dress and independence of their women. The Village Chenchus build their conical huts in a cluster near a hamlet. Bands of migrant castes camp in the nearby fields, and the tribal Chenchus from the surrounding forest come to Konduru to barter for goods. All of these people can be considered marginal: they do not share fully in the great traditions of Indian civilization, and they are not integral parts of a village that articulates members of many castes into a single functional whole.

Another group of people who form a community in the loosest sense of the term are the governmental workers assigned to the schools, post office, forest office, and block offices of Konduru. A few are local residents and members of their respective communities. Most are outsiders whose sole reason for living in Konduru is a government assignment. Some have left their families in distant hometowns. They associate with themselves and organize their own social activities. Transfers are frequent. For the most part they are strangers and officials and, hence, outsiders in the village.

HAMLETS, VILLAGES, AND TOWNS

People on the plateau, living in hamlets and villages, seek the fellowship and security of numbers. Women gossip at the wells and visit in the courtyards. Men toil together in the fields, citing their proverb, "Alone a man plows four fields with difficulty, in company he plows five with ease." At dusk they gather under a tree to discuss the affairs of the day.

Residence groups fall along a continuum, with hamlets on one end, cities on the other, and villages and towns in between. There is no sharp dividing line between stages, and all are linked by numerous ties with each other to form larger systems. However, the general characteristics of a residential group change as it increases in size.

Villages, being larger than hamlets, are also more autonomous. They are able to provide within themselves most of the social, political, religious, and even economic services essential to life during times of crisis, war, famine, and plague. Hamlets are dependent adjuncts of villages and consist of a few families residing apart from the village for specific reasons. As centers for agriculture and trade, villages have shops and markets that buy local produce and sell essential commodities. Within the village are found many of the basic service and specialist castes such as Ironworkers, Carpenters, Goldsmiths, Weavers, Tailors, Barbers,

lims, Shudras, and the two large Harijan castes have burial grounds of their own. Revered patriarchs, however, are frequently buried in their fields, near wells they had dug, or under trees they planted.

Hamlets, villages, and towns articulate local caste groups within the local structure. To understand the internal operations of these residential groups we need an understanding of the social forces that shape the behavior of their inhabitants.

CHAPTER FOUR

STATUS AND POWER

BEHAVIOR in Konduru is influenced by several factors: norms defined by social groups and communities, multiple relationships between participants, the control of various forms of power, and the psychological bent of the individual. While the first two factors set boundaries on what is acceptable behavior, the individual can maneuver considerably within these limits by using power. Naturally, some of his efforts will conflict with those of his fellowmen and result in competition or discord, while others will coincide with their efforts and lead to cooperation and alliances. Status and power are used by the villagers to pursue their goals. At first glance it might appear that these two are unrelated; but, men and castes acquire status through the effective mobilization of power, and social status provides access to new avenues of power.

THE STATUS STRUCTURE

Status hierarchy and structured interaction lie at the heart of the caste system. They provide the formal contexts within which, as Carstairs notes (1967:61), the villager acts with a sense of security, poise, and assurance. In their absence, the villager is often insecure and vacillating.

Pollution

The social status of men and castes is closely related to the concepts of pollution as these apply to physical contact, sexual contact, and food and water. Certain material objects, such as dead bodies, blood, human excreta, and liquor, are considered defiling and those who handle them rank low. Pollution also is thought to spread from polluted men to the pure. While observance of practices regarding body pollution is rapidly disappearing in such public places as the marketplace, schools, and buses, its vestiges remain in the temples and, even more so, in the homes of the higher castes.

Food and water are important symbols indicating rank within Konduru. High castes refuse defiling foods such as meat and strong drink. Moreover, each caste refuses water or cooked foods that have been handled by those ranked below themselves. To accept either from the hand of another is to acknowledge the equality or superiority of the giver. Exceptions are fruit and *pakka* foods (those rendered pure by being fried in rendered butter) which can be exchanged within limits.

Village wells, as sources of water, become status symbols. Each community, if possible, has its own well, and wealthy families have their own private wells in their courtyards. Only where water is extremely scarce, as on the eastern end of the plateau, do all share a common well. Even then different pulleys may be delegated to different communities. Problems do arise as can be seen by the plight of the Maradpur Weavers who moved their hamlet onto a rise beside the Chenchu settlement in 1965. Lacking a well of their own at the new site, the Weavers came to the Chenchus for water. The Chenchus would not permit the Harijans to draw water from their well; hence, the Weavers had to wait each morning by the well until the Chenchu women could fill their pots. In return, the Weavers gave the Chenchus an annual gift of clothes. In recent years, however, government regulations declaring that public wells are open to all have begun to cause changes.

From comments made by Konduru informants, it is clear that caste ranking is perceived largely in terms of the readily observable symbolism of food exchange. Commensal patterns for the Konduru castes as given by six older informants showed minor disagreements, but there is general accord on the significant patterns (see Tables 6, 7). First, it is clear that clusters of castes which mutually exchange food and water appear at different social levels. There is no single ladder with each caste occupying a separate rung. Second, castes occupying essentially the same social position and competing for higher rank often refuse each other's food. Third, Muslim informants claim that they are not bound by the food restrictions of the Hindus and will eat food pre-

Table 6. Distribution of Specific Social Practices According to Caste[a]

Caste	Food Consumption				Customs				Days of Pollution	
	Intoxicants	Mutton and Fowl	Pork	Beef	Cross-Cousin Marriage	Widow Remarriage	Sacred Thread	Cremation	Birth	Death
Brahman	−	−	−	−	−	−	+	+	11	11
Ayyavaru	−	−	−	−	−	−	+	+	11	11
Merchant	−	−	−	−	+	−	+	+	21	16
Craftsman	+	−	−	−	+	−	+	+	11	10
Tambali	+	−	−	−	+	−	+	+	11	10
Kapu	+	+	+	−	+	+	−	+	21	10
Munnur	+	+	+	−	+	+	−	−	11	10
Herdsman	+	+	+	−	+	+	−	−	21	10
Potter	+	+	+	−	+	+	−	−	11	10
Winetapper ...	+	+	+	−	+	+	−	−	21	10
Gypsy	+	+	+	−	+	+	−	−	−	−
Washerman ...	+	+	+	−	+	+	−	−	11	10
Barber	+	+	+	−	+	+	−	−	21	10
Turk	+	+	−	+	+	+	−	−	41	
Weaver	+	+	+	+	+	+	−	−	21	10
Leatherworker .	+	+	+	+	+	+	−	−	11	10

[a] Note: + practiced, − prohibited.

pared by anyone (although in no instances was it observed that they took food from the hands of Harijans).

The unique position of the Panchala or artisan castes also becomes apparent. These five castes interdine as a block but neither accept nor give food to the higher castes. Low Shudra informants and some Harijans assert that until the last two decades they too refused to touch food prepared by the Panchala. The explanation appears to be a historical one. According to inscriptions of the eleventh century, the Panchala lived outside villages as polluting castes. Under the Chola kings they received the rights to blow conchs and beat drums at their weddings — rights formerly denied low castes (Hassan 1920:546). In recent times they have gained recognition as high Shudras throughout parts of Andhra Pradesh, but this rise in status has not apparently led to a comparable change in commensal patterns.

Changing times are having effects on the food habits of the citizens of Konduru. Better roads and bus service have opened the door for new ideas and products from the outside world. Moreover, those trav-

Table 7. Food and Water Exchange Patterns for Selected Konduru Castes[a][b]

Givers →

Receivers	Brahman A	Brahman B	Merchants	Goldsmiths	Carpenters	Ironsmiths	Temple Asst. A	Temple Asst. B	Farmer A	Farmer B	Herdsmen	Potters	Courtesans	Gatherers	Chenchu	Earthmovers	Winetappers	Gypsies	Washermen	Barbers	Soothsayers	Quarrymen	Rockcrushers	Turks	Cottoncarders	Weaver Priests	Weavers	Leatherworkers
Brahman A	*	-	-	-	-	-	-	-	-	-	-	-	-	-	-	-	-	-	-	-	-	-	-	-	-	-	-	-
Brahman B	-	*	-	-	-	-	-	-	-	-	-	-	-	-	-	-	-	-	-	-	-	-	-	-	-	-	-	-
Merchants	+	+	*	-	-	-	-	-	-	-	-	-	-	-	-	-	-	-	-	-	-	-	-	-	-	-	-	-
Goldsmiths	-	-	-	*	+	+	-	-	-	-	-	-	-	-	-	-	-	-	-	-	-	-	-	-	-	-	-	-
Carpenters	-	-	-	+	*	+	-	-	-	-	-	-	-	-	-	-	-	-	-	-	-	-	-	-	-	-	-	-
Ironsmiths	-	-	-	+	+	*	-	-	-	-	-	-	-	-	-	-	-	-	-	-	-	-	-	-	-	-	-	-
Temple Asst. A	+	+	+	+	+	+	*	-	-	-	-	-	-	-	-	-	-	-	-	-	-	-	-	-	-	-	-	-
Temple Asst. B	+	+	+	+	+	+	+	*	-	-	-	-	-	-	-	-	-	-	-	-	-	-	-	-	-	-	-	-
Farmer A	+	+	+	+	+	+	+	+	*	-	-	-	-	-	-	-	-	-	-	-	-	-	-	-	-	-	-	-
Farmer B	+	+	+	+	+	+	+	+	+	*	-	-	-	-	-	-	-	-	-	-	-	-	-	-	-	-	-	-
Herdsmen	+	+	+	+	+	+	+	+	+	+	*	-	-	-	-	-	-	-	-	-	-	-	-	-	-	-	-	-
Potters	+	+	+	+	+	+	+	+	+	+	+	*	-	-	-	-	-	-	-	-	-	-	-	-	-	-	-	-
Courtesans	+	+	+	+	+	+	+	+	+	+	+	+	*	-	-	-	-	-	-	-	-	-	-	-	-	-	-	-
Gatherers	+	+	+	+	+	+	+	+	+	+	+	+	+	*	-	-	-	-	-	-	-	-	-	-	-	-	-	-
Chenchu	+	+	+	+	+	+	+	+	+	+	+	+	+	+	*	-	-	-	-	-	-	-	-	-	-	-	-	-
Earthmovers	+	+	+	+	+	+	+	+	+	+	+	+	+	+	+	*	-	-	-	-	-	-	-	-	-	-	-	-
Winetappers	+	+	+	+	+	+	+	+	+	+	+	+	+	+	+	+	*	-	-	-	-	-	-	-	-	-	-	-
Gypsies	+	+	+	+	+	+	+	+	+	+	+	+	+	+	+	+	+	*	-	-	-	-	-	-	-	-	-	-
Washermen	+	+	+	+	+	+	+	+	+	+	+	+	+	+	+	+	+	+	*	-	-	-	-	-	-	-	-	-
Barbers	+	+	+	+	+	+	+	+	+	+	+	+	+	+	+	+	+	+	+	*	-	-	-	-	-	-	-	-
Soothsayers	+	+	+	+	+	+	+	+	+	+	+	+	+	+	+	+	+	+	+	+	*	-	-	-	-	-	-	-
Quarrymen	+	+	+	+	+	+	+	+	+	+	+	+	+	+	+	+	+	+	+	+	+	*	-	-	-	-	-	-
Rockcrushers	+	+	+	+	+	+	+	+	+	+	+	+	+	+	+	+	+	+	+	+	+	+	*	-	-	-	-	-
Turks	+	+	+	+	+	+	+	+	+	+	+	+	+	+	+	+	+	+	+	+	+	+	+	*	+	+	+	+
Cottoncarders	+	+	+	+	+	+	+	+	+	+	+	+	+	+	+	+	+	+	+	+	+	+	+	+	*	+	+	+
Weaver Priests	+	+	+	+	+	+	+	+	+	+	+	+	+	+	+	+	+	+	+	+	+	+	+	+	+	*	-	-
Weavers	+	+	+	+	+	+	+	+	+	+	+	+	+	+	+	+	+	+	+	+	+	+	+	+	+	+	*	-
Leatherworkers	+	+	+	+	+	+	+	+	+	+	+	+	+	+	+	+	+	+	+	+	+	+	+	+	+	+	+	*

[a] + = accepts, - = does not accept.
[b] Reproduced by permission of the *American Anthropologist*.

57

eling away from the village face the problem of finding suitable food. In the past a few poor high-caste men served meals in their courtyards for a small fee. The orthodox brought or begged foodstuffs which they prepared themselves. Today one finds tea stalls and restaurants (called hotels) in most villages. Travelers can usually find a Brahman Hotel where vegetarian food is prepared by Brahmans, a Reddi Hotel run by the highest of the meat-eating castes, and possibly a hotel run by Muslims. Travelers from Konduru, for the most part, frequent such eating establishments.

Changes in the political structure have raised other problems. Some of the high government officials of the plateau, including the Member of the Legislative Assembly (MLA) of the state, are Harijans. On their visits to Konduru the local headman, a Brahman, must entertain them. The problem is resolved by having vegetarian and nonvegetarian meals prepared by Brahman cooks and served in the local government office building. In this way, the headman's home still remains sacrosanct.

Other forms of pollution influence the daily routine of the individual. Menstruation and childbirth are thought to defile a woman and, to some extent, members of her household. During such a time she cannot cook or participate in normal social or religious activities. When, in 1964, the wife of Konduru's priest went into confinement, the annual Rama fair was delayed for several days. Death is also considered defiling for members of the household.

Caste Ranking

A man's status is closely related to his place in the caste hierarchy. Various attempts have been made to reach an objective ranking of castes in an Indian village (Srinivas 1955, Mayer 1956, Marriott 1960 and 1968, Freed 1963, and Hiebert 1969). Of the various techniques proposed, Marriott's was used to analyze caste ranking in Konduru. Thirty castes, all of them well known to the residents of Konduru, were selected for comparison. Most of these were represented in and around Konduru itself. Fifty adult males, selected by random sample from the 1962 voters' list of the village, were chosen to rank these castes. From those selected, forty-two were present in the village and were able to respond.

The names of the thirty castes were written on cards and each informant was asked to rank the castes in order of their position in the village. Illiterate informants were asked to rank each new caste as it was paired with those already sorted until its relative place was determined. Equivalence was noted whenever an informant treated two or three castes as equals. Two Muslim informants did not rank the Muslim castes, because they felt these castes did not belong to the caste system. Other Muslim informants included their castes in the general order. To check consistency over a period of time, the same test was given to eleven of the same informants a year and a half later.

An analysis of the data shows that a clear rank hierarchy of castes does exist.* Freed's suggestion (1963) was followed and each caste was paired with every other caste and the number of instances in which each was ranked higher was noted (see Table 8). The binomial test was used to locate significant breaks, and lines were drawn to separate the castes into groups of castes sharing essentially the same status. Nine such groups appear.

From a comparison of the statistical data obtained by Marriott's technique with the food exchange patterns and other behavior patterns observed in the village, it seems that the caste hierarchy should not be viewed as a single scale along which all castes are ranked. Rather, castes seem to belong to different sets, each having a clear internal rank order. It has already been noted that the Muslims and the Panchalas are most clearly understood as separate social subsets. On the basis of local myths linking the Harijan Leatherworkers to the Panchalas and the assertion by a few aged informants that these are all left-hand castes (possibly referring to the fact that the left hand is defiled and subservient to the right), we are probably justified in including the Leatherworkers with the Panchala. Likewise, the transient castes, who share only minimally in the Hindu social system and relate only marginally to its hierarchy, should be set apart. When these subsets are treated separately, the sharp distinction between upper High Shudras and lower High Shudras becomes apparent (see Figure 7).

* A Friedman's Chi Square of 986 was calculated for the rank distribution. This is significant well above the 99th percentile. For the binomial test the level of significance, alpha, was set at 95 percent and a two-tailed test was used. The critical scores for rejecting the null hypothesis that there is no rank difference between a pair of castes are 28 and 27 for $N = 42$ and $N = 40$ respectively. Ties were omitted and critical scores were calculated for the number of actual ranked pairs. This procedure involved only the Panchala castes. For the field data and a detailed analysis see Hiebert (1969).

Table 8. Matrix of Opinions on Caste Rank in Konduru[a]

	(1)	(2)	(3)	(4)	(5)	(6)	(7)	(8)	(9)	(10)	(11)	(12)	(13)	(14)	(15)	(16)	(17)
BrahmanA (1)	35/7	42/1	42/–	42/–	42/–	42/–	42/–	42/–	40/–	42/–	42/–	42/–	42/–	42/–	42/–	41/1	41/1
BrahmanB (2)		41/1	42/–	42/–	42/–	42/–	42/–	42/–	40/–	42/–	42/–	42/–	42/–	42/–	42/–	41/1	41/1
Merchant (3)			39/3	40/2	36/6	39/3	39/3	42/–	38/2	42/–	42/–	42/–	41/1	41/1	42/–	41/1	41/1
Goldsmith (4)				19/23	24/18	23/2	28/2	35/14	36/7	41/6	42/–	42/–	42/–	42/–	42/–	41/1	41/1
Farmer A (5)					21/21	26/16	26/16	16/14	28/–	14/–	39/3	42/–	42/–	42/–	42/–	41/1	41/1
Temple Asst. A (6)						19/23	20/13	22/9	29/–	33/–	38/4	39/3	42/–	42/–	41/1	41/1	42/–
Ironsmith (7)							12/9	26/16	30/12	31/11	34/8	36/6	37/5	42/–	42/–	41/1	41/1
Carpenter (8)								27/15	31/11	35/7	37/5	38/4	38/4	42/–	41/1	41/1	41/1
Temple Asst. B (9)									26/16	26/16	34/8	35/7	38/4	32/10	33/9	39/3	42/–
Farmer B (10)										23/19	30/12	36/6	36/6	38/4	34/8	37/5	42/–
Herdsman (11)											29/13	35/7	36/6	40/2	36/6	38/4	42/–
Tribesman (12)												21/21	21/17	25/17	25/13	29/8	34/4
Potter (13)													23/9	16/20	20/16	22/15	26/22
Gatherer (14)														28/14	22/20	20/15	22/17
Winetapper (15)															38/5	27/15	20/27
Courtesan (16)																40/2	40/4
Earthmover (17)																	14/11

HIGH SHUDRA

MID SHUDRA

60

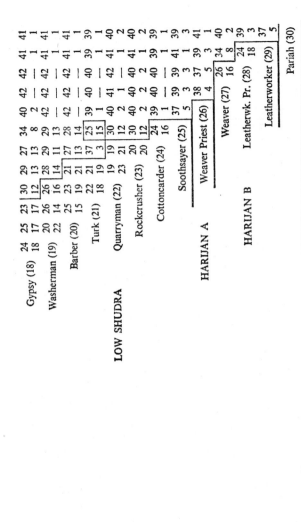

LOW SHUDRA

HARIJAN A

HARIJAN B

NOTES:

Code numbers in parentheses and corresponding caste names refer to both the column under which the number is centered and the pair of rows in front of which the name and number appear.

Row caste is ranked higher than the column caste in the number of instances shown by the upper number. Column caste is ranked higher than row caste in the number of instances shown by the lower number.

Lines are drawn between scores showing a significant difference in rank and those that do not. Major divisions in the social order are marked by heavy lines between the column/row headings. Caste groups containing more than a single caste are labeled to the left.

[a] Reproduced by permission of the *American Anthropologist*.

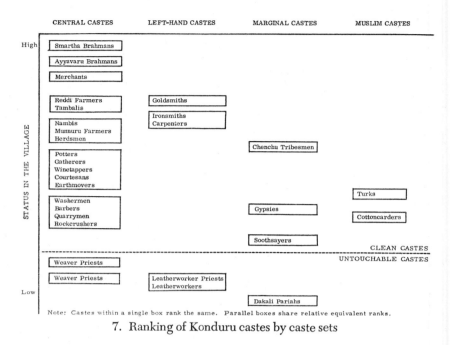

Note: Castes within a single box rank the same. Parallel boxes share relative equivalent ranks.

7. Ranking of Konduru castes by caste sets

There was a high rate of agreement among subjects on the rank order of the castes, and the retests given them eighteen months later showed considerable consistency over time.* There was disagreement about the rank of Muslims. Hindu informants of all levels equated them with the Low Shudras, but the Muslim informants unanimously placed themselves on a par with the Mid-Shudras. To a man, the six Barbers considered themselves higher than their rivals, the Washermen. To a man the five Washermen placed themselves above the Barbers.

Individual Ranking

One might ask whether within a caste system there is no room for the individual to raise his status. The caste system has been char-

* To test whether informants applied essentially the same standards in ranking the castes, a Kendal Coefficient of Concordance was calculated for the rank scores. The results, " = .85, showed a high rate of agreement among rankers (W ranges from 0 to +1). To check consistency over time, the same test was given to eleven of the same informants a year and a half later. The retests were compared with the original tests by using the Kendal Rank Correlation Coefficient. The average correlation for the eleven informants was $\tau = .81$, which shows considerable consistency over a period of more than one year.

acterized as static and rigid by Cox, Simpson, Yinger, and others (Berreman 1960). Keesing observes (1966:282): "But segmentation and stratification may have crystallized to such an extent, and become so reinforced by religious and other sanctions, that competition has been eliminated and the whole system has become immobilized in terms of status and personnel. Such a fixed system is labeled a *caste*." Although the rigid nature of caste has been refuted by Srinivas (1952), Berreman (1960), and others, the idea of its existence persists. Bohannon writes (1963:168): "At the other extreme from a situs system of rank is the caste system, where the social range of the rank is total; that is, an individual's caste position affects every aspect of his life, and he occupies the same rank in all the intercaste organizations to which he belongs."

It would seem from observations in the village that there is some flexibility for the individual to acquire status outside of his caste standing. Such noncaste factors as wealth, education, leadership abilities, and age are not completely ignored, at least not within the village where the individual is known and judged in his own right. The question might be asked, to what extent, if any, do noncaste factors influence a man's personal rank in the village. To find an answer to this question, Marriott's technique was used to rank eighteen well-known men of Konduru. These men were selected on the basis of caste, wealth, and offices held so that there would be representatives of leaders and ordinary men from each of the major levels of the caste order (see Table 9). While this method of selection results in an unusually large sample of leaders, it does provide the contrasts which test the effect of caste and noncaste factors on individual status. The same forty-two informants were asked to rank these eighteen men on the basis of their influence in the village. Villagers speak of this as *mārta* (a man's word), in referring to a man's influence in such affairs as caste and village councils.

When techniques were used similar to those applied to caste ranks, four status groups were evident from the data (see Table 10): village headman, village priest, high-caste elders, and general villagers.* The last group includes a broad range of ranks including several stragglers at the bottom.

* The Friedman's Chi Square for the rank order of men was 560, which is significant well above the 99th percentile. The critical scores remain the same as those for the caste rank tests.

Table 9. Castes, Occupations, Offices, and Land Possessions of Persons
Ranked Listed in Order of Their Caste Ranks[a]

Person	Caste	Occupation	Office	Acres of Land
Balayya	Brahman A	Priest, farming	Family priest and guru	40
Krishna Chari	Brahman B	Priest, farming	Village headman, temple priest, Pres. of Naya Panchayat	60[b]
Peddayya	Merchant	Moneylending	Caste headman, richest man in the area	17
Balaswami	Merchant	Small shop, farming		10
Lalayya	Goldsmith	Smithing, farming	Village philosopher	9
Sayanna	Temple Asst. A	Farming, assistant priest	Priest in Hanuman shrine	2
Narayya	Ironsmith	Smithing, farming	Village architect, herbal doctor	42
Kondayya	Temple Asst. B	Tea shop, assistant priest	Priest in Hanuman shrine	18
Lingayya	Farmer B	Farming	Village panchayat clerk	32
Sambayya	Herdsman	Herding, farming	Caste elder	31
Pullayya	Winetapper	Farming, wine contracting	Caste elder	33
Lakshayya	Washerman	Washing clothes, farming	Caste headman	24
Bakayya	Barber	Begging, village drunkard		—
Allaudin	Turk	Farming	Headman of Muslim Turks	25
Ikbal	Turk	Assistant in mosque, government worker	Assistant in mosque	6
Rangayya	Weaver	Farming	Harijan Weaver headman	13
Yellayya	Weaver	Day labor, poor Harijan		1
Pentayya	Leatherworker	Leathercrafting and farming	Leatherworker headman	5

[a] Reproduced by permission of the *American Anthropologist*.
[b] Of this, 56 acres belong to the Rama temple as trust lands.

From comments made by informants during the test, it became clear
that Krishna Chari (Brahman B) ranked above Balayya (Brahman A)
largely because of his influence as the acknowledged headman of the
village. Within the period of traceable history, this office has circulated
among different Brahman castes in Konduru. Yet more than caste is

required to gain the office. A man must have the ability to unite people, to provide leadership, and to help settle village disputes peaceably. Other Brahmans in the village own more land or money, yet have less influence in village affairs. As the acknowledged headman, Krishna Chari controls the indigenous village councils, and as elected chairman of the recently formed village Naya Panchayat, he controls the formal political structure.

Table 10. Matrix of Opinions on Individual Rank in Konduru Village[a]

```
Krishna Chari | 39 40 42 40 42 42 42 42 42 42 42 42 42 42 42 42 42
              |  3  2  —  2  —  —  —  —  —  —  —  —  —  —  —  —  —
       Balayya   30 28 32 31 42 39 42 42 40 41 42 40 42 42 42 42
                 12 14 10 11  —  3  —  —  2  1  —  2  —  —  —  —
         Lalayya   23 25 22 42 39 41 40 41 42 40 40 41 42 42 42
                   19 17 20  —  3  1  2  1  —  2  2  1  —  —  —
          Peddayya   23 26 41 37 41 41 41 41 40 40 40 41 41 41
                     19 16  1  5  1  1  1  1  1  2  2  1  1  1
            Narayya   22 42 39 41 41 42 42 40 41 41 42 42 42
                      20  —  3  1  1  —  —  2  1  1  —  —  —
             Lingayya   41 35 40 40 42 42 40 41 40 42 42 42
                         1  7  2  2  —  —  2  1  2  —  —  —
               Pullayya   18 26 23 | 28 28 26 28 31 40 38 41
                          24 16 19 | 14 14 16 14 11  2  4  1
                 Allaudin   21 26 26 | 32 30 32 37 42 42 42
                            21 16 16 | 10 12 10  5  —  —  —
                  Sambayya   24 29 28 27 | 31 32 41 41 42
                             18 13 14 15 | 11 10  1  1  —
                    Sayanna   22 25 25 22 | 37 39 39 42
                              20 17 17 20 |  5  3  3  —
                   Lakshayya   21 24 26 | 30 39 38 41
                               21 18 16 | 12  3  4  1
                        Ikbal   24 22 29 | 39 38 42
                                18 20 13 |  3  4  —
                    Balaswami   21 | 32 35 40 39
                                21 | 10  7  2  3
                     Rangayya   26 | 42 36 42
                                16 | —  6  —
                      Kondayya   27 | 36 37
                                 15 |  6  5
                        Pentayya   23 | 28
                                   19 | 14
                        Bakkayya   25
                                   17
                          Yellayya
```

NOTES:
   Individual names refer to both the column under which the name appears and to the pair of rows on which the name is centered.
   Row individual is ranked higher than the column individual in the number of instances shown by the upper number. Column individual is ranked higher than the row individual in the number of instances shown by the lower number.
   Lines are drawn between scores showing a significant difference in rank and those that do not. Heavy lines between names mark statistically significant breaks in the rank order.

[a] Reproduced by permission of the *American Anthropologist*.

The third category of men consists of high-caste leaders. It includes those active in the local village government together with the village philosopher and the Vaishya moneylender, who is the richest man in the valley. Included in the main body of general villagers are leaders of the Low Shudra, Muslim, and Harijan castes, as well as common high-caste merchants and priests. Trailing behind are the Harijan commoners. It is noteworthy that Rangayya, acknowledged spokesman for the Harijan Weaver caste, has a rank equivalent to a twice-born Vaishya merchant and two High Shudra priests and significantly above the Low Shudra village drunkard.

There was less overall agreement among informants for personal ranks than for caste ranks.* Moreover informants showed less consistency in ranking individuals over the period of a year. It would appear from this that personal rank is more fluid than caste rank.

A Model of the Status Structure

A comparison of caste and personal ranks can give us some insight into the complex nature of status ranking in Konduru. It shows a surprisingly low correlation between a man's personal status and that of his caste.† Thus, even in a caste system, noncaste factors such as wealth, power, and leadership play an important role in determining a man's status.

A useful model for relating caste and noncaste statuses in the village can be found in vector analysis (see Figure 8). Caste and noncaste

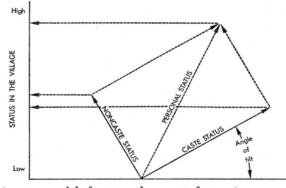

8. A vector model of caste and noncaste factors in personal status

* The Kendal Coefficient of Correspondence for personal rank scores was $W = .787$ and for caste rank $W = .848$. The mean Kendal Coefficient of Correlation for retests for personal rank scores was $\tau = .69$ and for caste rank scores $\tau = .81$.

† A Kendal Coefficient of Correlation was calculated for the scores of each informant, between the actual personal rank order and the predicted rank order of these people based on their caste alone (using the informant's own caste ranking data). The distribution showed a surprisingly broad range (.08 to .82), and the mean coefficient of correlation was $\tau = .514$ (τ ranges from -1 to $+1$).

statuses appear as the two dimensions in the social hierarchy. A man's personal rank is the sum of these two vectors. With this model it becomes clear how an influential Harijan can rank higher in the eyes of his fellow villagers than a disrespected Shudra and how he can be considered equal to an ordinary high-caste man (see Figure 9). Applied to the Hindu castes as a whole (see Figure 10), the model points out the complex nature of the status system in Konduru.

How do noncaste factors influence the status structure of the village?

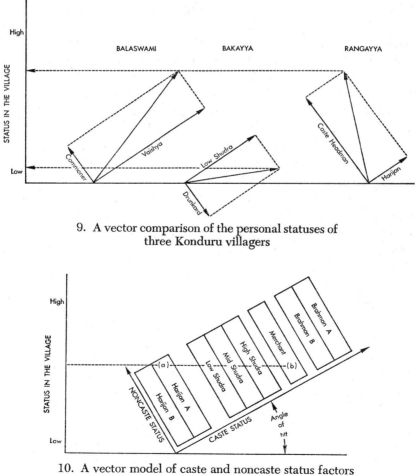

9. A vector comparison of the personal statuses of
three Konduru villagers

10. A vector model of caste and noncaste status factors
in Konduru village

A partial answer to this question can be found in an analysis of the manipulation of power in Konduru.

THE POWER STRUCTURE

In analyzing the role of power within Konduru, individuals and groups become the actors and the village becomes the stage. Men and groups in Konduru pursue their goals through effective mobilization and use of social power, which is the ability to influence social life. They gain this power by controlling limited resources needed by the society such as wealth, by controlling the offices that regulate communication or have the publicly recognized authority to make decisions for groups or the village as a whole, and by inspiring the respect and following of others. Each man's pursuit is resisted by others seeking the same power. Moreover, the village as a whole has certain rules or norms about how power may be sought. To be sure, the norms are neither the same for all of society, nor are they uniformly applied. Those who control power can bend the norms, but only for a time.

Power can be converted into privilege and privilege into prestige, which can thereby alter the arrangement of groups within the village. Those with prestige frequently have access to more avenues of power which they can use to perpetuate their privileged positions. Nevertheless, changes in the power hierarchy do occur as a result of external influences, new alliances, individual and group efforts, and the accidents of history.

Sources of Power

The acquisition of wealth, whether land or money, is an obvious source of power. Penury is the butt of much village humor and verse.

> A mother curses a penniless son, his father rejoices not in seeing
> him,
> His brother won't talk to him, the Washerman is angry with him,
> His son doesn't obey him, his wife will not embrace him,
> Even his friends avoid him for fear he will borrow more,
> By cash all may rule; therefore, my friend, get cash!

Wealth can be converted into prestige. Ideally this is done through generosity; the rich should feast the poor in the local temple, sponsor evening dramas in the village square, lend willingly to the poor, and give generously to beggars. Still greater merit is gained by restoring an old temple or erecting a new one. The value of generosity is exhorted in many village sayings such as the following:

> "One who gives food in times of famine [in summer when food
>   is scarce]
> One who gives money in times of plenty [in winter when cash
>   is scarce]
> One who is brave in times of battle,
> One who cheerfully pays his debts,
> To these four I bow," says Krishna.

But old men lament the modern spirit of the times which, they insist, is making men turn from gods to money. Goldsmith Lakshayya, Konduru's aged philosopher, expressed these sentiments in a poem:

> The man of plenty, who sees not the sufferings of the poor,
>   Will flounder in the sea of mammon,
> Like a dog that wallows in a heap of grain which he cannot eat.
>   Oh Kodanda Rama of Konduru.
>
> A covetous man keeps everything for his own stomach,
>   Who is there now who scatters unto others?
> The covetous are numerous, they multiply everywhere,
>   In this universe. Oh Kodanda Rama of Konduru!

For the most part, however, wealth is converted into prestige by the more direct means of controlling jobs and purchasing support. Increasingly, large rock houses, whitewashed walls, transistor radios, bicycles, watches, and pens are displayed as symbols of affluence. The wife of a well-to-do man does not need to work in the fields and also has servants to help her in the house.

Offices are another source of power. Some are hereditary such as those of the indigenous police officer, land recorder, temple priests, and de jure caste headmen. Others have been developed over the years by the people who have gained reputations for wisdom, impartial justice, and leadership. Highest of the indigenous Konduru offices is the village headman who organizes activities for Konduru as a whole, calls panchayats to settle difficult disputes, and receives visiting government officials. This office is assigned by village consensus to the high-caste man with the best leadership qualities and widest support. People still speak in awe of the previous Konduru headman, a Karnam, who was also the village land accountant. When he suddenly died in his prime (some say by poison from the hand of an enemy), the villagers increasingly turned to Krishna Chari with their problems. Krishna Chari is an Ayyavaru Brahman and a priest in the Rama temple. Throughout the plateau he is known for his sagacity, but some older men complain that he lacks the forcefulness needed to keep village order and unity.

There are others who participate in the indigenous village government: the police patel who is responsible for keeping order and reporting troubles to the headman and government police, the patwari or land officer who keeps land records and collects revenue, and the mali patel who assists in the collection of taxes. There are elders who have no official position but do have considerable power as mediators in village squabbles. Like the village headman, they earn their reputations by rendering impartial judgments and sound advice. The most important religious offices are those of *purohit* (the family priest who is summoned to perform rites in the home) and of the temple priests: both are hereditary. In addition, the Muslims and Christians traditionally have certain offices held by their own people.

To a great extent leadership in Konduru lies in charismatic men who, by their own personal qualities, attract and lead others. Strong castes are those with dynamic leaders. Strong villages have dominant castes or leaders who take the initiative. Usually, village movements are born of strong leaders and die with them, for the step from charismatic leadership to formal organization is uncommon. The situation with the temples is illustrative of this point. Periodically, inspired men lead a revival of worship in one of the many abandoned temples scattered about the plateau, as Krishna Chari did with the Rama temple of Konduru. So long as leadership is present, worship rites continue, but when the leadership is lost the shrine decays into oblivion as it awaits a new savior. This is the present fate of the local Shiva temple.

In small hamlets and in an occasional village, leadership may exist in a "dominant caste." Regarding dominant castes, Bailey (1960:258) writes:

Power is concentrated in the hands of the dominant caste. The main features of this system are well known and have been for many years. . . . One caste has direct control over economic resources and it alone has a corporate political existence: the other castes derive their living by a dependent relationship upon the dominant caste, and in themselves they have no corporate political existence. Their political relationships are as individual clients of a master in the dominant caste. Political ties run vertically in the system and not horizontally: political and economic rank tends to be consistent with ritual rank: the dependent castes are not all of equal rank but are organized in several grades, and this is apparent in ritual usage.

The dominant caste need not be the largest caste. By controlling economic and political power it may be able to dictate to other castes in the village and thus maintain harmony. Several types of dominant caste hamlets can be readily observed around Konduru. Caste-based hamlets have a single leading caste which may even be Harijan. Agricultural hamlets are frequently controlled by a few wealthy landlords.

The dominant caste concept needs modification, however, to fit the proliferation of castes noted for larger villages like Konduru. Dominance may continue, but power no longer rests with one specific caste. Rather it lies in a power block formed by the alliance of several significant castes (those which control sufficient power, either in terms of prestige or size, to enter actively into the struggle for power). In Konduru, for instance, there is no single caste that monopolizes land and finance, and seven castes are represented by more than thirty families. The members of the two Harijan castes are most numerous, but their low rank and relative poverty preclude their dominance. They are, however, useful allies to the Brahman-Merchant-Washerman alliance that controls the village.

Power is the right to act, by force if need be. The truth of this can be seen in the change that took place for the Muslims in Konduru over a period of years.

৬ ৬ When the Nizam ruled Hyderabad State, Konduru Muslims passed a rule that no processions should beat their drums or play music near the mosque or prayer wall. On one occasion the Muslims beat up Leatherworkers who ignored the rule, on another they stopped a high-caste procession that was taking the village gods to a nearby well for a bath. After independence was obtained, the Shudras decided to test the rule by staging a drama in the street beside the mosque. Although they beat their drums and played their instruments all night long, the Muslims did not appear; there was no Muslim government to back their demands. Now no one observes silence near the Muslim shrines. ৬ ৬

Power may also be *satyagraha* (force of truth), the nonviolent elicitation of public support for a cause. *Satyagraha* can act as a lever for the weak to use to right an injustice. Many different types of actions are undertaken in hopes of eliciting this type of public support. A man begins a fast unto death unless his quarrel is settled; another plagues the village elders until they take up his case; a creditor sits in the doorway of his powerful debtor until repayment is made. Beggars camp before the door and clang their bells, sing their shrill songs, pound their drums, strum their gourd guitars, or blow their horns until the incessant noise forces the residents to bring them a gift of grain or money. If they feel that the gift is not commensurate with the donor's wealth, they repeat their performance until they are satisfied. Local disciples of the Sarvodaya movement organized a mass meeting in Rameshvaram during the 1964 elections and shamed the three feuding candidates into forming a united front. In the fall of that same year, when land taxes were raised, farmers of the area organized sit-ins in the district government offices for several weeks.

The Use of Power

Power in Konduru consists ultimately in the ability to control people. The networks of relations within the village provide avenues whereby an individual can extend influence and control over others. Kinship and marriage are the primary sources of support. Castes, associations, economic and religious systems, and communities and villages encompass broader human groups.

Chains of support-obligation must be established and maintained if they are to be available when needed. Wealth can be used to gather debtors, and by extension, their followers. Generosity in sponsoring entertainment and public activities attracts yet others. Political offices can be exploited for personal gain or for the advancement of kinsmen and allies. Political associations may provide useful friends or may rob a foe of needed support. Even a priest can use his authority for personal advantage. Villagers still laugh over one *purohit* who took advantage of a rich but miserly merchant who was fulfilling the last rites of his deceased father. Apparently, the priest kept the son dipping in the ice-cold water of the well until the skinflint agreed to pay more for his services.

Power is often exercised indirectly through the channels of mutual obligation and referral. Lacking direct influence over another, a man must seek the support or recommendation of someone who does. For example, a Konduru teacher wanting to move failed to obtain a transfer in spite of three years of applications. When he persuaded a fellow casteman, a friend of the regional educational officer, to drop a few casual comments to the officer, the transfer was effected immediately. Relationships are not confined to messages of a single type such as friendship or an official transaction. Each can be used to communicate many sorts of messages, and in the process the relationship is compounded and strengthened.

In Konduru, relationships between two individuals are often compounded by increasing the number of bonds between them. A laborer soon becomes a debtor and a client to his master. Gluckman defines this overlapping of roles between the same persons as multiplex relationships.

In more differentiated societies a person is linked to a variety of different persons, with many of whom his relationship is formally confined to a single interest . . . It is chiefly in our simple family that we find the mixed ties that are typical of Barotse society. There nearly every social relationship serves many interests. . . . these relationships which serve many interests, I propose, for brevity, to call . . . *multiplex* relationships.

In Konduru the same people may be related simultaneously as kinsmen, religious participants, economic rivals, political leaders and underlings, and so on. Multiplex relationships intensify the ties linking individuals and provide a greater measure of interdependence and security.

Nowhere is the compounding of interdependence more obvious than in patron-client relationships. These may begin on a simple level, a farmer hiring a laborer or a workman taking on an apprentice, but they often become complex, even hereditary. Unlike contractual relationships where the responsibilities cease as soon as each party has fulfilled its part of the agreement, patron-client relationships are characterized by a mutual responsibility that enters all aspects of life. The patron becomes increasingly responsible for the total welfare of his client, to the point of providing school fees for the client's children, grain for festivals, annual gifts of clothes, gardening land, fodder, loans, and bail, in addition to wages. The client, for his part, reciprocates by being completely available to do the wishes of his master without thought of an equal exchange of time and money. For the client, this relationship provides security in times of need, as well as the reflected glory of his master; for the patron it provides support and power. Even beggars become clients to a generous man and claim their rights to receive a regular dole from him once he has given them a few gifts!

Indirect channels as well as multiplex relationships to achieve personal goals can readily be seen operating between rival politicians:

&&Pulla Reddi, a wealthy farmer, ran against Mulla Reddi, a rich moneylender, for the office of Sarpanch or chairman in the Maradpur Naya Panchayat (village council) in 1964. The selection was to be made by the eleven village representatives or *panches* who had been voted into office during the general elections. Seven of these were high-caste men who were split equally between the two candidates. The balance of power lay with the four Weaver representatives. Pulla Reddi called these four together and informed them that since he was their employer, he expected them to vote for him. Mulla Reddi had no direct way to pressure the voters, but he had lent large sums to the Weaver caste headmen of several villages. He summoned these leaders and asked them to order their men to support him. Now, the four Weavers were caught in the middle.

On the eve of the elections, the Weaver caste headmen sent last-minute representatives to pressure the voters. Seeing them come, Pulla Reddi called the local Weavers and demanded that they drive off the intruders, with the promise that no ill would befall them. With a will aided by the strong drink provided by their patron, the Weavers complied. Hearing of the riot, the headmen arrived and were also beaten by the local Weavers who were now quite drunk. The elections were canceled and the Reddis went to court to unravel the case.

The Weaver headmen could not accept the insult. They called a caste panchayat in a nearby hamlet and began to debate their course of action. Hearing of the assembly, the Maradpur Weavers panicked. If banned from the caste, they were doomed to social ostracism. They had no course but to send a delegation to apologize to the elders. After listening to their story, the elders finally agreed upon a fifteen-hundred-rupee fine plus food costs for the panchayat which had been meeting for three days. A few hours later the delegation returned with slightly over five hundred rupees which they had collected from their families and pleaded poverty. After a stern warning from the elders that, henceforth, no Weaver should be a pawn in the hands of the rich Reddis, the money was accepted and used to pay the expenses. The balance was spent on a skin of beer which was passed around to all as a symbol of reconciliation. ᛡᛡ

The four Weaver electors were economically obligated to Pulla Reddi, but socially subject to their caste elders. It was a question of caste ostracism or loss of jobs. Their response was typical. By siding with their employer at the outset, they reinforced their patron-client ties, since these would probably be harder to reconstruct should they break. But after the immediate crisis passed, they turned to renew their caste bonds, and no one, not even their employer, would expect them to further endanger their caste ties.

Conflict and Alliance

Rivalries and alliances are frequent themes in the village power struggles. Intercaste rivalries generally occur between castes of approximately the same rank, rather than those separated by a rank gap. Weavers and Leatherworkers are often bitter rivals, as are the Barbers and Washermen, the Reddis and Kamas, and the Shivite and Vaishnavite Brahmans. Conflicts that start as little arguments soon become matters of caste honor, a highly volatile issue. Such was the case when the Konduru Weavers fought the Leatherworkers.

ᛡᛡThe trail from the hamlet of Chintalonpalli, home of the Leatherworkers, to Kumarlonpalli, where the Leatherworkers go for earthen pots, used to pass through the Weaver hamlet of Kalmulonpalli. One evening in 1946, members of a Leatherworker wedding party set out with drums and a band to fetch the ceremonial pots needed in the rites. Beyond Kalmulonpalli the trail passed close to an open well where a Weaver was drawing water with a pair of newly broken oxen. When the oxen bolted because of the noise, the farmer threatened loudly to break the wedding pots and bring bad luck upon the wedding should the party disturb the oxen upon their return. On the way back, the Leatherworkers, caught up in the spirit of festivity, and showing their disregard for the Weavers, beat their drums harder and shouted a little louder. The oxen bolted again. The infuriated Weaver grabbed his stick and shattered one of the pots. There were shouts of rage and loud accusations before the Leatherworkers finally moved on.

The next evening a wedding party left to fetch the bride. Again they had to pass through Kalmulonpalli. Hearing of this, the Weavers decided to put the Leatherworkers in their place. All moved their beds and mats outside until the only street through the hamlet was clogged. At midnight the bridal party returned, only to find the road impassable. They shouted at the sleeping Weavers, but the Weavers refused to move. The Leatherworkers were few so they withdrew to take counsel. A messenger was sent to the Konduru police station and soon three constables arrived. Beds and bedding were thrown aside as the wedding procession marched triumphantly through.

The Weavers outnumber the Leatherworkers on the plateau almost two to one, and they were ready for a fight. The next day the Leatherworkers found their road north blocked. They retaliated by barricading the road through their hamlet along which the Weavers drive their cattle to graze in the forests to the south. The Weavers called in the Weaver Mashti who are known for their skill in handling sticks and clubs. The Leatherworkers brought in Leatherworker Mashti. The boundary between the hamlets was an armed camp. Small fights flared, but neither side dared to make an all-out assault. The local police tried to break the impasse, but with little success. The hostilities continued as the Leatherworkers went to court. To raise money, they sent messengers to the Leatherworkers in the surrounding districts to obtain contributions. The case dragged on for several months while the elders of Konduru and Harijan leaders from the plains tried to mediate a settlement. They pointed out the needless expense and suffering, as well as the fact that both hamlets would have to live together peaceably in the end. Weary of the struggle, both groups finally agreed to restore free passage and the case was withdrawn from court. ♫♫

Intercaste conflicts reaffirm caste ties over wider areas by calling on fellow castemen elsewhere to assist with donations. On the other hand, it is these castemen from distant areas who are not involved personally in the local dispute that want to see peace restored, since the continued levies are costly with no profit to themselves. The local leaders of other castes also want peace so normal village relations can be resumed. Eventually the parties reach a compromise which permits them both to live together in the same area.

Conflict is not always dysfunctional. When it does not threaten the social structure, it can reinforce group identity and delineate social boundaries. It can also lead to a reaffirmation of existing norms or give rise to new ones, besides providing release for tensions. Conflicts in a segmented society, though frequent, usually lack the characteristic divisiveness associated with conflict in closely knit societies. As Cozer notes (1964:154), "the multiple group affiliations of individuals make them participate in various group conflicts so that their total personalities are not involved in any single one of them." While breakdowns in social relations are frequent, they are generally temporary. Settlements, based on face-saving compromises aimed not so much at achieving absolute justice but at reaching workable agreements, are mediated by those who are not immediately involved, although they would be negatively affected by protracted disharmony. Moreover, there is honor in being known as a peacemaker. Until a settlement is reached, parties involved in the conflict revert to formalized relationships, which have a minimum degree of personal involvement, yet permit communications to continue.

Alliance is an effective way to increase power. Powerful castes seek allies from lesser castes. Rivalry between castes often results in shifting alliances. In Konduru, for example, the Brahman-Merchant power block finds support in the Washermen and Leatherworkers while their rivals, the Reddis, turn to the Barbers and Weavers. The interplay of rivalry and alliance was well illustrated during the Konduru elections.

⌇⌇During the decades before the 1964 elections, the Brahman-Merchant alliance dominated politics on the plateau with the exception of a few hamlets controlled by the Reddis. Reddis, on the other hand, controlled much of the surrounding plains. Matters changed when Venkat Reddi led a Reddi attempt to gain power. He organized a local branch of the Congress party with the support of the district Congress leaders, many of whom were Reddis. Krishna Chari, Konduru's headman and incumbent Sarpanch, and his supporters had always considered themselves part of the Congress party but had never bothered to organize a local branch. When Venkat threatened to run against Krishna Chari in the upcoming elections, the village leaders tried to avoid a showdown.

Krishna offered Venkat the post of assistant Sarpanch but Venkat was not content with anything less than being the top man.

In previous elections Krishna had always filed in the eighth ward which resulted in his uncontested victory. But Konduru had been redistricted by an outside government official (whom the local leaders charged with gerrymandering), and the eighth ward now had a preponderance of Barbers who sided with the Reddis. Krishna, not daring to lose face in a village election, refused to file for office in that ward. His supporters tried to find a seat where he could file and be uncontested. Of the thirteen wards, eight were reserved — two for women, five for scheduled castes or Harijans, and one for tribals. Furthermore, many of the high-caste wards were assigned reserve seats. Only five general seats were left, and most of them in wards controlled by Harijan voters. Village leaders finally went to the Leatherworker hamlet of Chintalonpalli and persuaded the Harijan elders there to support Krishna. Under orders from the caste elders the two Leatherworkers contesting the seat withdrew and Krishna was elected without opposition.

Venkat, for his part, filed in the third ward against three other contestants. He was careful to file two applications, each signed by one local man who supported his candidacy, for in some elections the applications had been challenged. If opponents kidnapped or bribed the nominating man, and he failed to show up to identify his signature within the time limit, the candidate would be removed from the race. In a hotly contested election Venkat won by a small margin.

The Brahmans and Merchants controlled nine *panches* in the newly elected Naya Panchayat, while the Reddis only controlled four. Krishna was elected Sarpanch and Venkat received no office at all.

Intercaste rivalry did not cease here. Sarpanches of the Achampet Community Development Block gathered to form the Samiti (area council) and elect a Samiti president. Until 1964 the plateau had had its own Samiti with Krishna Chari as the president. Now the Konduru Samiti had been merged with the Achampet Samiti and Krishna had to compete with the Reddi leaders of the plains led by Tirupathi. Krishna did not want to challenge the widespread Reddi power, but the Brahmans, Merchants, and dissident Reddis persuaded him to represent them and to seek the office of the Samiti president. Krishna could count on the support of ten of the Sarpanches out of the thirty-three who would elect the president. To win, he would need at least seven more, some of whom would have to be Reddis from the plains. Krishna found further support in an alliance with Gopal Reddi. Gopal had been Samiti president in Achampet for some years but had been deposed by Tirupathi Reddi through some technicalities. Now he was seeking revenge. Krishna and Gopal met frequently for strategy councils and visited disgruntled Reddi electors who might be persuaded to vote against Tirupathi. Both parties kept their movements secret, and each had its spies out to watch the movements of its opponents. Once it became clear that Tirupathi would have a majority of the electors, those who were vacillating were quick to join his party. In the end he combined wealth and Reddi power to win a decisive victory. &&

Power and Change

Power as used in daily life is a shifting commodity. When it runs counter to the social structure, tensions develop that must be resolved. As Bohannon points out (1963:369), such strains can be eased by either readjusting the components of the system or changing the system itself. The Barbers used their power to readjust the social order when they fought for the right to use any pulley at the village well.

&&When the clean castes of Podur dug a village well, they put up three pulleys: one for use by the Merchants, one for the Washermen, and one for the other clean castes. But as the Barbers grew in strength and numbers, they chafed at the restriction since they did not want to share the third side with all the others.

In 1963 the Barbers decided to test their strength. While the rest of the Barbers hid behind a nearby mud wall, one began to draw water at the Merchant pulley. When a passing Merchant grabbed the bucket and demanded to know who had given him this privilege, the Barber picked up a stick and struck the Merchant on the head. The hidden Barbers appeared ready for a fight, but the Merchants, fewer in number and noted for their cowardice, hid behind bolted doors. The subinspector of police (S.I.) heard of the incident and came to investigate. Only after the Barbers gave him two hundred and fifty rupees did he withdraw charges. But the Barbers won their point — now all clean castes may draw indiscriminately from the well. The Merchants come early before the others appear. &&

To the analyst the caste structure and the power structure provide complimentary models for analyzing patterns of village behavior. In the former the village is seen as a single functional whole in which men and organizations, as parts, work together to achieve such mutual goals as survival and security. In the latter it is seen as an aggregate of individuals and groups, each with a measure of autonomy, pursuing their own goals within the limits set by the village acting as a whole. To the villager the caste structure and the power structure provide alternative courses of action. In the former he subordinates himself to the norms of the caste society, in the latter he seeks to further his own prestige by using other courses of action. The two structures are not mutually exclusive. Prestige gained in one can be converted into the other. Part of the strength of the village lies in this flexibility within the social structure which enables it to adapt to the changing fortunes of life.

CHAPTER FIVE

NETWORKS

OVERLAPPING groups in Konduru bind men into a system with ties of multiple loyalties and dependency which bridge the social rifts of caste. Other powerful forces that reinforce these bonds are networks of enduring relationships between specific individuals or families, which provide each with certain rights and obligations in respect to the other. While the raison d'être may be based upon caste monopolies, the relationships themselves do not link caste groups but individual families. Such networks provide a man with channels for exercising power and generate participant audiences that are concerned with his affairs. Three types of networks, jajmani, begar, and debt, illustrate the general characteristics of these patterned relationships in Konduru.

JAJMANI

First studied in detail by Wiser (1936), jajmani has more recently attracted considerable interest (Gould 1958, 1964, Beidelman 1959, Harper 1959, Leach 1960, Sarma 1961, Orenstein 1962, Pocock 1962, Bhowmich 1963, Rowe 1963, Saraswati 1963, and Orans 1968). As Beidelman notes, the essence of the system is the cultivation of land and the distribution of its produce. Underlying his and other discussions, however, is the assumption that high castes control the land and serve as jajmans or landlords while low castes provide the workers. But what happens, as often occurs, when the landholder belongs to a low or untouchable caste and his workmen come from equal or higher castes? The answer to this provides some clues about the essence of the jajmani system.

Land ownership is at the center of the jajmani system. Bordered by ample lands, Konduru lacked until recent decades the intense land pressures characteristic of much of the surrounding plains. As a result, low-caste folk obtained land in considerable quantities (see Table 11). Most farms are small; eleven percent are less than two acres. A few high-caste farmers with large farms of over fifty acres control eight percent of the agricultural land. There is little absentee farming. While the high castes tend to have larger average holdings per farmer (Brahmans average thirty-eight acres and Leatherworkers four and a half), they by no means control a major portion of the land. Brahmans and Merchants own less than one-tenth of the soil. Shudras own almost two-fifths and the Harijans own at least one-third.

Jajmani links farmers or jajmans to craft and service castemen (*kamins*) in a hereditary system of mutual dependence (see Figure 11). The nature of the relationship varies with the rank and wealth of the jajman. Between Harijan jajmans and Shudra *kamins* the relations are economic, but between high-caste jajmans and their workers there are numerous social and ritual ties as well.*

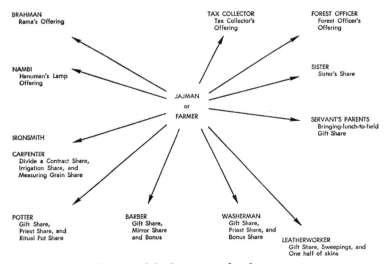

11. Distribution of the harvest under the jajmani system

* In the past the model for the jajmani system was the petty village kingdom ruled by the *zamindar*. Konduru villagers still refer to the village rulers as the big jajmans or lords. These rulers could call upon the services of any villager and in turn were responsible for the ultimate welfare of the village and its inhabitants. All major sections of the village had parts in the rituals of the court and all sought the largess of the ruler.

Table 11. Land Distribution in Konduru Mauza Village

Caste	Number of Land Holders	Percent of Land Owners in Each Caste according to Size of Land Holdings in Acres					Average Size of Holding in Acres	Total Land Holdings by Castes	
		0 to 5.0	5.1 to 10.0	10.1 to 20.0	20.1 to 50.0	50.1 Plus		Acres	Percent
Brahman	13	30.7	0	0	38.6	30.7	38.3	498	4.7
Merchant	18	16.8	22.2	27.7	33.3	0	16.2	293	2.8
Reddi farmer	29	20.8	6.9	24.1	37.9	10.3	24.0	696	6.6
Mumur farmer & Maden farmer	109	24.8	22.0	24.8	27.5	.9	14.0	1528	14.5
Artisan	11	27.2	36.5	27.3	9.0	0	11.4	126	1.2
Herdsman	40	27.5	30.0	25.0	17.5	0	11.4	459	4.4
Kuruva	31	51.6	29.0	12.9	6.5	0	6.7	205	2.0
Gatherer	45	33.3	28.9	28.9	8.9	0	9.3	421	4.0
Winetapper	29	58.7	17.2	13.8	10.3	0	6.8	197	1.9
Potter	49	42.8	24.5	24.5	8.2	0	8.9	440	4.2
Chenchu	21	38.2	28.6	33.2	0	0	7.2	111	1.0
Gypsy	11	27.3	27.3	9.0	36.4	0	14.0	154	1.5
Washerman	25	36.0	44.0	12.0	4.0	4.0	10.4	260	2.5
Barber	12	8.3	50.0	33.4	8.3	0	10.1	121	1.2
Misc. Shudras	15	13.3	33.3	40.1	13.3	0	12.8	191	1.8
Muslim	108	43.5	24.0	17.6	13.0	1.9	10.8	1169	11.1
Weaver	381	35.5	34.1	23.8	6.6	0	8.5	3260	31.0
Leatherworker	78	64.1	23.1	12.8	0	0	4.9	379	3.6
Total	1025							10,508	
Percentage of total land area		9.8	21.2	29.3	31.6	8.1			

High among Konduru's *kamin* craftsmen are the Ironsmiths, who claim to have come to Konduru as a single family during the era of the zamindars and to have been granted the jajmani rights of the village at that time. From scrap iron purchased from traveling merchants they make and mend the agricultural implements of the farmer. In addition, for a small fee, they make chairs, beds, door frames, oxcarts, and other equipment to serve village needs. A few decades ago when the Ironsmiths could no longer meet the labor requirements of the expanding village, they called in an outsider and gave him certain patrons on lease. He agreed to take only the harvest payments as his share of the remunerations and to turn over all fringe benefits to the original Ironsmiths. Since then the first Ironsmith family has multiplied. When the heirs laid claim to the leased work rights, the newcomer refused to acknowledge the claims. The heirs, who could no longer forcibly demand their rights, blame their situation on the times. Said one of them, "In the past justice and order ruled and no man could have taken our rights. Now men have no respect for authority." Actually the Ironsmiths are split by rivalries and cannot unite to enforce their rights. On the same level are the Carpenters, who claim descent from a single ancestor called Great Carpenter who was summoned by the zamindars and given the carpentry rights of the village. Today the two Carpenter families maintain one hundred and fifty plows under the jajmani system. Others are serviced by the Ironsmiths, who also do woodwork. Farmers bring wood, cut in the nearby forests, which the carpenter then dries and seasons. Using an adz, a plane, a chisel, and a hammer, he shapes a plow, harrow, or other farm tool.

In their hamlet, Kumarlonpalli, near the clay pits, ceramists of the Potter caste prepare the earthenware used by the farmers for cooking, eating, and storage. For a small price they also provide the ceremonial pots needed at all major festivals and family rites.

Washermen do the village laundry. They call at clean-caste homes and take the clothes to a stream, where they are soaked in lime water, baked over low fires, beaten on the rocks to loosen the grime, and rinsed. After drying on the surrounding bushes, the clothes are ironed and returned to the owners. Harijan farmers, on the other hand, must bring their laundry to the stream and immerse it in water before the family Washerman will handle it. Later they must call for it at the Washerman's house. Washermen are sometimes accused of wearing their patrons' clothes before returning them. Citing a local proverb, "The Washerman's finery is never his own," villagers charge him with calling at the homes of his richest clients whenever there is a wedding in his family in order to get some fine clothes in the laundry to wear at the festivities.

The Barber is the village gossip. He calls at the clean-caste homes with his little metal box of knives, brushes, soap, and mirrors. There he shaves the farmer, cuts his hair, trims finger and toe nails, pulls teeth, lances boils, and performs other minor surgery. He must take care to dispose of the clippings properly lest the jajman's enemies use these in destructive magic against their owner. Not quite in jest the people say, "There was a burglary at the Barber's house last night; three pots of combings were stolen!" Barbers do not go to Harijan homes; however, the Harijans use the Barbers' tools in return for a small share of the harvest.

A patron's Leatherworker, using leather that he has tanned, makes and repairs shoes for the family, harnesses for the oxen, and leather spouts for the irrigation buckets. He and his family are called upon to help in planting, weeding, and harvesting the crops. Often close ties develop between a jajman and his Harijan clients.

Harvesttime brings the jajmani relationships to sharp focus, for it is around the threshing floor that all those who have had a share in raising the crop gather to share in its bounty. A wealthy high-caste jajman is lord as he presides over the distribution of the golden grain — the product of a season's labor — heaped upon the freshly swept threshing floor. The first portions are sent to the family priest and the temple as offerings (*dhānam*) to the gods and to the village officials in respect for their authority. Then the laborers receive their portions in order of their rank. Craftsmen have come for their contractual shares or *gutha*, a term that implies their independent and essentially equal status. Service castemen and Harijans receive *biksham*, or gift shares, which signifies their dependence upon the benevolence of their patron. At times the pile is small and all face the coming year with anxiety, for the harvest represents food, the central concern of life. There will be other jobs and earnings, but these will be needed for buying clothes, paying debts, and arranging weddings. In other years the harvest has been generous and all rejoice in their prosperity.

The Ironsmith and the Carpenter come forward first to obtain their shares. Together they divide contract shares, one share for each plow that they have maintained throughout the year.* If the harvest is rice, they also divide one pot of unhusked grain called the *arikkulli*, or irrigation share, for there is more wear on plows used in irrigated fields. In addition, they can demand the *ogaru* pot, or bonus share, given for measuring out the harvest onto the threshing floor. But this share is taken only if the harvest has been good and the farmer is well-to-do. For the irrigated crops a small bonus may be claimed if the rice was watered from small reservoirs since such watering entails little toil, but this portion is seldom demanded of a farmer who has spent long hours before dawn drawing water from an open well.

The Potter takes a gift share — one or two pots of grain — for providing the household pots throughout the year. There is a ritual measure consisting of a little grain, liquor, and money for the special pots needed by the master in his rituals. Finally, as priest to some of the field goddesses, the Potter receives a priestly portion (*numula kuntar*) and parts of the sacrificial animals.

The family Washerman collects a gift share for laundering the patron's clothes. Using a winnowing fan he measures out from four to eight scoops of grain, depending upon the number of adults in the jajman's house. He takes an added heaping fan of grain, the *poli cherta*, for priestly services: at seed time and again at harvest, after the first grain has been sent to the Brahman as a sacrifice to the temple gods, the Washerman brings offerings of grain and blood to the goddesses of the field and well. He also sprinkles some on the threshing floor and along the borders of the field to satisfy evil spirits. Finally, he runs around the freshly stacked sheaves of grain waving aloft the last bundle shouting "poli! poli!" to celebrate the successful ingathering of another crop. The Washerman may also claim a bonus. As others look on he pulls away a small pile of grain until the jajman objects. The Washerman complains of the extra work during the past year and of the master's many guests and then pulls out a little more. The master scoops some back, while noting the scarcity of the harvest and the delays in getting the laundry, which was not clean even then. Since

---

* Each contract share for the Ironsmiths and Carpenters consists of two pots of grain. Pots vary somewhat in size. On the average a pot holds about eleven liters.

there is a participant audience present, neither dares press his demands too far.

Washermen have other duties. After births and deaths there are defiled clothes to be cleaned and messages to be delivered to kinsmen. In preparation for marriage ceremonies, he whitewashes the master's house and helps erect the pandal in the courtyard, besides laundering clothes for the family and guests. He delivers wedding invitations and, during the ceremonies, has the right to carry the torches or lamps in the many processions. But weddings are not all work. During the festive days he fills up on rich wedding foods, and after it's over he takes home the hulled rice used in the rituals as well as other gifts. If his jajman is rich, he may even hope to receive the gift of a calf or a cow.

The Barber measures out a gift share, four to six fans of grain, for shaving the household males and a *poli cherta* for ritual performances. He pulls aside his bonus (*addam dōsili*) "for showing the mirror" to his prosperous masters so they can have the privilege of observing their tonsure while it is taking place. Since the poor do not give a bonus at harvesttime, they are shaved without the benefits of soap or a mirror. The Barber does more than shaving, however; his knife is used at births to sever the umbilical cord while his wife assists in the delivery of the child. After funerals he shaves his clients at the time of their purification. But it is at weddings that he is most needed. He prepares the groom and is given small gifts of grain, liquor, coins, and the clothes that the young man had been wearing. He pares the nails of the couple during the ceremonies and claims the unhusked rice used in making the ritual designs. He arranges for a Barber band to play for the ceremony and also for the many processions that welcome the bridal party, that fetch the ceremonial pots and sacred earth, that accompany the wedding party to the temple, and that parade the newlyweds through town. Finally, on an auspicious day fixed by the family *purohit*, the Barber performs the ritual tonsure and receives the groom's turban as a symbol of his assumption of the jajmani rights over the new home.

When the Shudras have taken their share, the Leatherworker approaches for his: a gift share of a half pot of grain for repairing shoes and harnesses and a share for repairing the irrigation bucket at the well. He also claims the meat and one-half of the skins of the jajman's cattle that die throughout the year. The other half of the skins he must tan and return for the jajman's use. After the grain is cleared from the threshing floor, the Leatherworker sweeps up the tailings as his bonus (*danda kaṭṭu*). The biggest reward of the harvest often goes to the Leatherworker who has been a faithful worker during the past year. Such a man helps in the field work by drawing water before dawn to irrigate the rice, by sleeping in the fields to protect the harvest from wild pigs from the surrounding forest, and by guarding the cut grain from thieves. He beats the large leather-covered drum in his master's processions and sleeps before his door at night. The jajman rewards such a servant with a generous portion which can amount to ten pots of grain.

Still others lay claim to the harvest. First fruits are sent to the family *purohit* as an offering to the gods. The Nambi takes all he can raise in cupped hands for the daily lighting of the lamps to Hanuman, the monkey-faced god. The village patwari must be given some rice from irrigated fields and extra cash after taxes are paid, and the Forest Officer expects a small gift. Parents who bring lunches to their hired son in the field can claim the *ambali gasam*. Sweepers who clean the yards and house have their share. Even the jajman's sister has rights to a basketful of grain which she may store in her brother's house for times of need. As Ironsmith Narayarna said, "Some politicians come and say we should be communists. When the harvest comes, the birds, the rats, the wild pigs, the Carpenter, the Washerman and Barber, the Potter, the field workers, the gods and priests, the government officials, the beggars and bards, and our own relatives all come for a share. What is this, if not communism?"

Just as important as the harvest distribution in the jajmani network are the fringe benefits, the many informal exchanges of goods and services throughout the year. A prosperous jajman permits his workers to build houses on his land and to cultivate small gardens rent free. At times of religious festivity he gives them clothing and grain for a feast. He provides them with fodder to tide their cattle over a dry summer and with manure for their gardens. Above all, they look to him for cash loans to carry them through times of crisis.

Relationships between a jajman and his workers are often close. They frequently address him as "father," and he may respond with "son." His clients take up arms for him in power struggles and assist him in the elaborate rituals that bring prestige to a family. In return they reap a measure of security. Big Lakshayya, headman of the Konduru Washermen, said, "In years of plenty we can earn more by contracting work elsewhere, but in years of plenty no one suffers anyway. It is in times of crisis, when drought sets in, that a man can turn to his jajman and find help."

Secondary relationships develop between craft and service caste families. Washermen wash clothing for Barbers, who in turn cut the Washermen's hair. Similar exchanges link Washermen families with families of Ironsmiths and Carpenters. Barbers, whose occupational monopoly has begun to weaken, no longer exchange work with these last two castes. Introduction of aluminum utensils has undermined village dependence upon the Potter and other clients no longer exchange labor with Potters.

The jajmani system assumes two forms: one is introverted (see Figure 12) and the second is extended (see Figure 13). In the first, a

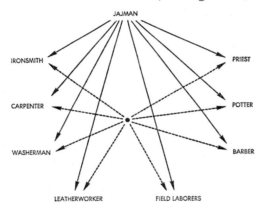

—————— Primary ties between a Jajman and his workers
- - - - - Secondary ties between the workers themselves

12. Model of an introverted jajmani network

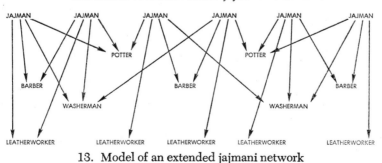

13. Model of an extended jajmani network

powerful landlord or a small number of related landlords have a group of clients who are completely within their service; they work for the jajman, his clients, and workers. Several of Konduru's hamlets consist of just such introverted jajmani groups. In the second, each jajman is served by clients from different castes, and each client serves many masters. One Konduru Barber has work rights over more than a hundred houses, and five others serve more than fifty. A number of Washermen have rights over at least fifty families. Where clients are not dependent upon a single jajman, they command a degree of independence not found in the introverted system.*

Various mechanisms are used to maintain a balance between supply and demand for skilled labor. During the era of the village kingdoms, petty kings and zamindars sought out workers in surrounding areas and attracted them with promises of land work rights. According to caste myths, this method was used by the Konduru zamindar to bring in the present lineages of Barbers, Washermen, Ironsmiths, and Leatherworkers. If members of a caste already reside in the village, they seek help by arranging an adoptive marriage for a daughter or by calling in kinsmen to help. Outsiders who intrude upon the monopolies of a local caste without invitation face open hostility and even attack. Faced with a labor surplus, some men use adoptive marriages or an invitation to move to areas of scarcity, while others take up day labor, salaried positions, or agricultural work — jobs that are open to anyone. The following incidents illustrate the dynamics of jajmani work rights.

დ დ Five generations ago, after its defeat by the zamindar of Siddapur, there were no Washermen in Konduru. When Sanjeeva Dharma Rao II restored community life, he found two Washerman brothers in Jadcherla and offered them land and the work rights of Konduru. From these two sprang the dominant lineages of Konduru Washermen. Two sons of one of the founding patriarchs had too much work and they called in their sister's husband and gave him a portion of the laundry rights. His descendants, known as the Buttons, have lived in Konduru now for more than four generations, yet they are looked down upon by members of the dominant lineage, who constantly remind the Buttons of the generosity of their forefathers.

* Compare the case of the Trespassing Washerman in Chapter Three with the case of the Rival Politicians in Chapter Four.

The Barbers tell a similar tale. When the Lord of Miryal Guda, near Hyderabad, came to visit the Lord of Konduru, he brought along his train of servants. Among these was a Barber called Red Fellow. Since there was too much work for the single Konduru Barber, Big Barber by name, the Konduru zamindar asked his friend to let Red Fellow stay and marry one of Big Barber's daughters. In return Red Fellow received one-third of the village work rights as his portion. A curse rested upon the lineage of Big Barber. His son and grandson each had only single male heirs, so that people began to say "Big Barbers have only one son." A second man, summoned to marry the granddaughter of Big Barber, was given rights over four of Konduru's hamlets and six acres of land. A third married Big Barber's great-granddaughter and received two hamlets and four acres of land. Only in the fifth generation, the present, has the Big Barber lineage branched into three families. In the meantime, the descendants of Red Fellow, founder of the Marbles Lineage, multiplied. Red Fellow had two sons, one of whom obtained the work rights of Podur. The other had numerous descendants so that there are now nineteen heirs to his portion. ৬৬

Tensions within the jajmani system are not uncommon, and both parties have patterned ways of expressing discontent. The jajman withholds or delays payments, refuses loans, or treats his worker harshly. Although the client does not strike, for then he could lose his position, he stages a work slowdown and does a poor job. A jajman can fire his client, but he then faces the difficult task of finding a replacement. The client's fellow castemen, for the most part, will neither take the job nor permit outsiders to do so. There is often little recourse for the jajman other than to take the client back and find a workable settlement. A disgruntled jajman can complain to his client's caste leaders, who will then try to find a solution to the problem. Washerman Lakshayya explained the procedure: "When one of our men does a bad job and his master complains, we tell him he must do a better job or our caste will have a bad reputation. Sometimes, if trouble continues, we arrange an exchange. We give the complaining master to the Washerman's brother or relative in exchange for another, but we are careful to make an equal trade; otherwise there will be more trouble."

The jajmani system serves many purposes. It relates landowners and laborers in the production and distribution of economic essentials. The jajman should not be equated with the clean castes, nor should it be thought that the system depends upon a few wealthy jajmans or a shortage of workers as some suggest. The exchange of goods and services is not always equitable, but villagers do not perceive the procedure in terms of the contractual exchange of equal values — rewards are measured in more than economic terms. As Rowe points out (1963) jajmani also serves as a credit system. A poor laborer can get loans from his wealthy jajman for life's emergencies. On the other hand, the small farmer is assured of essential services without paying for them until the harvest is in. Finally, the division of labor provides an avenue whereby ritually pure, high-caste farmers employ workers of less pure castes to perform defiling tasks in the field and home. This is, however, more a function of caste than of jajmani, for high castemen outside jajmani networks depend upon the same castes to perform similar tasks.

BEGAR

Begar is a system that links families of certain castes to the village in a network of hereditary government service (see Figure 14). Begaris, or workers, are required to perform certain tasks for the village in exchange for the right to use certain gift lands called *innam bhōmi*

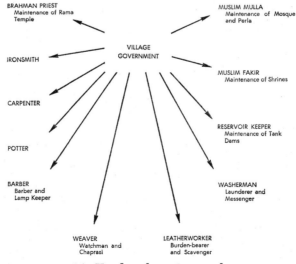

14. Konduru begari networks

(see Table 12).* In the old days, according to Konduru's aged men, the village lord was responsible for seeing that all essential services were available. Carpenters, Ironsmiths, Potters, Barbers, Washermen, and others were brought in and given jajmani and begar rights. Begaris were reportedly taken to the local temple and "married to the village." Today begar is dying out, but it still functions in Konduru in a limited fashion.

Table 12. Begar Tasks and Gift Land Holdings according to Castes in
Konduru Village in 1965

Caste	Begar Tasks	Gift Lands in Acres	
		Dry	Wet
Brahman	Maintenance of the Rama Temple	55.8	0
Muslim	Maintenance of Mosque and Perla	120.9	0
Muslim	Maintenance of Mahbub Swami Shrine	5.8	0
Telugu	Maintenance of reservoir dam	19.6	3.2
Weaver	Maintenance of reservoir dam	12.7	2.7
Carpenter	Carpentry	19.3[a]	0
Ironsmith	Metal work	21.0[a]	0
Potter	Providing pots	10.2[a]	0
Barber	Barbering and caring for lamps	101.9[a]	0
Washerman	Washing clothes and serving as messengers	62.1[a]	0
Weaver	Watchmen and chaprasis	40.0	0
Leatherworker . . .	Burden bearers, cleaners, wood gatherers, and water drawers	75.0	0

[a] Twenty-five percent of the crop is paid as tax to the government.

Leatherworker begaris attend government officials passing through on duty. When an official camps outside the village, the begaris show up to draw his water, collect firewood, and, in general, serve his needs. At his departure they carry his luggage to the next village. They also carry chains for the survey teams and perform tasks for the local government. These services entitle them to the use of seventy-five acres of gift land. Twenty-three Weaver families currently share begar rights as village watchmen and messengers. One or two men sleep before

* In anthropological terms this arrangement is called usufruct — the right to use an object of property without possessing a title of ownership to it. *Innam bhōmi* in the past could not be sold. The holder had full rights to till the soil himself or to rent it to others so long as he fulfilled his begar tasks. Moreover, these rights were inherited by a man's sons, if they assumed the begar obligations. The ultimate title of the land, however, remained with the village. In 1965, there was a movement in the legislative circles to give full title of gift lands to their holders, but no actual decisions were made at the time.

the houses of the village officials at night while others patrol the village and report disturbances to the police patel. Passing officials use them to summon individuals for private audiences or to announce public meetings in the village square. In the past other caste services were needed: Washermen to launder the clothing of passing officials, Barbers to cut their hair and trim their lamps, Potters to provide cooking utensils, and Ironsmiths and Carpenters to furnish the necessary furniture and tools. These, too, have gift lands.

The village government is responsible for the maintenance and use of the three earthen dams, which were erected across nearby streams to store water during the monsoon season. These reservoirs supply water to a few fields and to the small stream flowing beside the village which is used for washing clothes, bathing, purification rites, and watering cattle. A family, having begar rights, supervises each dam and controls the irrigation water by orders from the patwari, who is also kept informed of any leaks that could threaten the dam. Gift lands have also been set aside for the religious leaders who maintain the Rama Temple, the Mosque, and the Mahbub Swami Shrine.

During an era when many governmental functions took place on the village level, the begar system served a vital role. It provided essential services for the community and integrated the government with the caste and economic systems of the village.

DEBT

For many in Konduru, to live is to borrow money. A village proverb is, "Big debts, aging, adultery, theft, poverty, illness, and irregular meals; these are man's greatest troubles." As Epstein has noted (1962), debt structures in southern Indian villages tend to be pyramidal. At the bottom are the poor who must arrange for small loans from creditors only a little more prosperous than themselves; these creditors, in turn, borrow from the wealthier men above them. Most of the villagers are debtors and creditors at the same time. At the top of this multitiered structure are a few rich moneylenders who use their capital to exploit the credit market (see Figure 15).

Small loans are needed for day-to-day emergencies, but large sums are required for weddings. Ironsmith Narayana noted, "There are three important events in a man's life: his birth, his marriage, and his death. At the first he is too young to celebrate, at the last he is not around, so a man must make the most of his wedding." A proper wedding, one which wins respect, in many cases costs at least a year's wages. Men spend years paying off marriage debts and some are still paying for a parents' wedding.

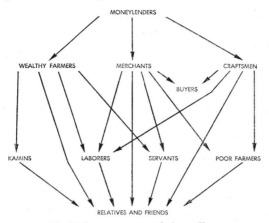

15. Debt structure of the village

Moneylenders, generally Merchants with surplus wealth, lend for profit and their interest rates are often high, up to fifty percent on short-term loans. But usury is not the only problem debtors fear. Many are illiterate and their creditor has the only record of the transactions. A few take copies of current transactions to another Merchant, who, for a few cents, will check them. Adages express their general fears. "The moneylender keeps the accounts; only God can read the script." Or, "When the moneylender borrows from you, he writes the account on the whitewashed wall [then it is easily rubbed out]." Mothers tell their children how misers bury their wealth under their beds and how thieves dig through mud walls to steal it. In the hot summer nights the children, sleeping in the yard, look up at the four stars of the Big Dipper (Ursa Major) and see the four posts of the Merchant's bed beneath which lies buried gold. Nearby the three thieves are creeping up to steal it.

Creditor-debtor relationships, however, involve more than purely economic transactions: there are numerous social overtones. They establish new patron-client ties or reinforce old ones. Creditors ask their debtors for support in the village power struggles but pay no additional remuneration. Jajmans lend money to their workers in order to lay first claim to the worker's time for the seeding and harvest when labor is short. On the other hand, debts may strain — even break — the bonds between kinsmen and friends. This possibility is pointed out in many village maxims.

> A man who leaves big debts is his son's enemy,
> A son who has no learning is his father's enemy.

> Learning in a book, a treasure lent to others,
> These are not there when needed.
> Such learning is not learning.
> Such wealth is not wealth.
> For use, keep cash in hand;
> For application learn lessons by heart!

Debts, like a man's possessions, are inherited by his sons and grandsons. But the collection of these debts can be a problem. It is said that in old times a creditor would camp on the doorstep of his debtor and starve himself until the debt was paid. Although a debtor exhibiting contempt for his creditor did not fear him in life, he did fear him in death. Spirits of those who die with unfulfilled desires are thought to return to earth to satisfy their cravings. A barren wife comes to catch children, an unrequited lover to claim his love, a miser to plague his money, and a creditor to demand his due. But the collection of debts can have more immediate and earthly dangers as was so with the Gypsy creditor.

&&The day after the Gypsy died in 1964, everyone in Konduru was discussing the case. Reportedly the wealthy Gypsy from the plains had given a sizable loan to an influential Reddi farmer of Podur who, later, had not wanted to pay it back. When the Gypsy arrived to collect his due, the Reddi arranged that he be arrested on charges of vagrancy. (Gypsies have a reputation for thievery throughout the area.) The Gypsy was taken to the Konduru jail for questioning. The subinspector of police was away, and others tried to extract a confession. The Gypsy refused to acknowledge any crime. He died the next morning. No one mentioned the loan when the police came to investigate. &&

Other problems can arise in settling accounts, as was the case when the farmers from Podur borrowed grain from a Konduru merchant.

ራራTen farmers from Podur came for peanut seed to Merchant Subramanyam of Konduru who agreed to loan them the seed if at harvesttime they would return fifteen pots for every ten they borrowed. After
the harvest was in, the farmers went home and, using the pot they
had used to check the original loan, measured out the amount they
owed. But when the peanuts were measured out before Subramanyam
and his servant, the farmers were short three pots. They argued that
they had carefully measured the peanuts before coming. Subramanyam
declared he would accept only his own measure. The farmers, after
examining his pot, demanded that he produce the old pot with the
copper patch which had been used to measure out the loan. Subramanyam refused to do so and ordered them to pay up or leave. The
debtors spent the day haggling in front of his house but in the end
they had to pay him the extra amount. They could have sold their
peanuts and paid him in cash, but at harvest prices are low; hence,
they would have lost even more. They paid, but in a way they got
their revenge for soon all knew of the Merchant's miserliness.ራራ

Konduru merchants lend cloth and foodstuffs to villagers during the
difficult days preceding the harvest and collect their share after the
crop is harvested. Before important festivals, traveling salesmen sell
clothing on time to the poor who have no credit in the village. Their
interest rates are higher, but their risks are also greater. Cattle merchants from the plains to the east come through Konduru each year
with large white-humped cattle which the farmers prefer to the local
nondescript breed. Prosperous farmers purchase the large cattle on
credit — a third down and the balance upon their visits in the next
two years. There is also a warranty, if the ox dies from disease during
the first year the farmer owes nothing more.

Indentured service, in which loans are repaid by work, is an arrangement accepted only by the poorest.

Too poor to support his large family, Leatherworker Pullayya
borrowed one hundred fifty rupees from Kotayya, a prosperous farmer.
To pay off the debt he sent his son Bukayya to work as Kotayya's
servant. Bukayya arrived early each morning to water the cattle, split
wood, and carry water. He helped in the fields and took his turn
guarding the crops from the wild pigs which came from the nearby
forest at night. Relations between Kotayya and Bukayya were good,

even friendly. Kotayya gave his servant meals, cigarettes, shoes, and two sets of clothes a year. In winter he gave Bukayya a long black shepherd's blanket woven from goat wool, a prized possession used as a shelter in storms, and a bed at night. He also agreed to finance Bukayya's forthcoming marriage on the condition that Bukayya serve him a few more years. ଓ ଓ

Ties between creditors and debtors are similar to those linking patrons and clients. Men find themselves in networks of obligations linking them to others across the boundaries of caste and community.

CONTRACTUAL EXCHANGES

Not all the economic functions are served by socioeconomic networks based primarily on status, to use Henry Maine's terminology. Contract plays a major role in Konduru. Trade is carried on by numerous small shops lining the main street. From their array of tins, boxes, glasses, and drawers, merchants dispense an astonishing variety of basic commodities: grain, cooking oils, spices, lentils, paper, pencils and pens, betel nuts, soaps, safety pins, and the like. Purchases are often small: a single cigarette, a postage stamp, a single pica's worth of cloves. Larger shops handle ironware, buckets, rope, flashlights, and kerosene. There are four cloth shops and a dozen tailors, a licensed liquor shop handling whisky imported from Hyderabad, and a beer parlor at the edge of town where men sit in the shade and quaff palm beer spiked with opium. Two restaurants appeal to high-caste vegetarians and nonvegetarians, respectively. Tea shops, pan stalls, and street vendors hawking sweetmeats, spiced edibles, and fresh fruit clutter the main street. Down a nearby alley the butcher displays his fresh meat.

The sleepy activities of the bazaar change on market day. On Tuesday nights merchants arrive on buses, carts, cycles, and foot to set up shop on blankets spread out on the main street. Some hawk cloth by the yard; others display ready-made clothing. There are stacks of aluminum pots, baskets of fruit, racks of books and piles of spices, trinkets, bracelets, and decorative mirrors. More traders arrive on Wednesday, together with the villagers and farmers who come from nearby villages to sell, buy, or just look and visit. By nightfall many of the merchants have left for the next village in their marketing circuit.

Table 13. Distribution of Work Patterns of Specialist Castes in Konduru

Caste	Total Number of Family Heads Examined	Caste Vocation Only		Caste Vocation, Some Farming		Farming, Some Caste Vocation		Farming Only		Other	
		Number of Men	Percent of Men	Number of Men	Percent of Men	Number of Men	Percent of Men	Number of Men	Percent of Men	Number of Men	Percent of Men
Barber	17	9	52.8	3	17.7	3	17.7	1	5.9	1	5.9
Washerman	27	5	18.5	12	44.5	9	33.3	1	3.7	0	0
Carpenter	2	0	0	2	100	0	0	0	0	0	0
Ironsmith	6	0	0	6	100	0	0	0	0	0	0
Goldsmith	4	2	50	2	50	0	0	0	0	0	0
Tailor	3	3	100	0	0	0	0	0	0	0	0
Total	59	19		25		12		2		1	

At harvesttime, merchants sally forth to surrounding villages to purchase the surplus crops. These are stored for sale during the dry season or are shipped by truck to the large market at Jadcherla on the railroad line.

Many villagers lack jajmani work rights (see Table 13). They together with those who have no caste monopolies often contract their services to others. Villages distinguish between three types of hired labor, each having its own prestige value. The lowest is coolie or day labor. The units of time used in calculations are not hours and parts of hours, but full and half days. Men hire out to plow fields, thresh grain, and stack fodder on high pole racks away from the white ants. They build houses and dig wells. Women transplant rice, cut the ripe grain, and work in the homes. A coolie is paid in cash except for harvest work which must be paid for in grain. Salaried labor (*jētham*) is more respectable, particularly if it is a government appointment such as a peon, a constable, or a teacher. Salaried jobs provide a measure of security and, over a period of time, often lead to patron-client type relationships where a newcomer settles in the village. Job contract (*gutha*), the most respected of the three types of employment, implies a degree of independence on the part of the contractor. A price is agreed upon after lengthy bargaining, and an advance must generally be made before the job is begun.

Status is giving way to contract in Konduru. The old men lament the passing of the old economic orders, for many of them cannot understand the new ones. But, the young feel more at ease with the new changing order.

CHAPTER SIX

PANCHAYATS

THE people of Konduru differentiate sharply between their own government administered by the leaders of their castes and village and the external government enforced by the many officials who frequent the village. Officers from many state and national programs, such as revenue, police, education, forestry, agriculture, and community development, come and go; however, they are rarely part of the village and its networks. Through the centuries villagers have seen external governments rise, flourish, and fall. Rajas, maharajas, emperors, nizams, zamindars, jagidars, and village lords have set up kingdoms, great and small, only to have them replaced by others. In the past villagers have often learned to expect through these governments only the heavy hands of taxation and conscription. It is only in recent decades that distrust for the external government has begun to lessen as villagers become involved in the democratic processes of their country. Traditionally they have depended upon their own legal systems to provide order and justice: the village walls provided safety and its leaders, though often autocratic, gave the people a government they understood. Now the kings are replaced by the state government of a modern India. Aspects of the old village systems still remain, however, and continue to serve important functions in Konduru affairs.

THE NATURE OF PANCHAYAT

Panchayats are the heart of Konduru's indigenous government. In one sense they are hard to define for they lack a neat organizational structure that lends itself to formal analysis, since panchayats are

101

more a procedure for reaching consensus than an institution for determining legal decisions. The membership is undefined and the rules unwritten. For the most part, they are temporary groups organized to solve specific problems. Yet there is a structure, one of process and order rather than organization and form, concerned with how to act rather than who may act. These traditional panchayats discussed here must be differentiated from the Naya Panchayats or village councils instituted by the Indian government under the Community Development programs which will be discussed later.

Panchayats operate on several levels. On the caste level they are used to settle caste affairs and internal disputes. Not all castes, however, have their own panchayats; many have so few members in Konduru that they operate as large families with family heads settling matters through informal discussions. Other castes like the Konduru Merchants, Winetappers, and Barbers are split into factions and do not function as single bodies. Only a few of the Konduru castes — Washermen, Weavers, Leatherworkers, Turks, and Cottoncarders — have functioning caste panchayats. In addition, some have hereditary caste gurus or religious leaders who belong to a superior caste within the same cluster or to a priestly caste. Such gurus have their specific territories and visit Konduru periodically to instruct clients in caste myths and customs and to pass judgment concerning chronic disagreements. Panchayats also operate on the village level by settling disputes between men from different castes, by working out discords that caste leaders are not able to take care of, and by dealing with matters involving the village as a whole.

Initial attempts to settle controversies that have become disruptive are made by informal panchayats. One of the disputants or an interested bystander calls the attention of a caste or village elder (*pedda*) to the situation. He in turn summons other elders, who are men of publicly acknowledged wisdom and leadership. Literally speaking there should be five, but the term *panch* (five) is also used in a general sense meaning a full and adequate number (a man who has "fed five" has put on a generous feast). In fact, the number runs from two or three for informal panchayats to more than fifty in some formal sessions. The elders hear the complaints and try to mediate a settlement. Success adds to the prestige of the elders and results in a cheap settlement for the contestants, while failure means the case goes to the caste or village headman and a more formal panchayat.

Caste headmen are generally the oldest men of the senior lineages in a caste. The village headman is a charismatic leader with high-caste status and some power who has earned the respect and the following of the villagers because of his impartial justice and leadership. Such leaders have the authority to call formal panchayats at which all major lineages or factions must be represented. The advice of headmen carries considerable weight, but they cannot pass judgment by themselves. Their leadership is a function of their ability to bring the assembled elders to some common consensus which will have the support of all or most of the major factions involved. If they fail to do this, their decisions are ineffectual, for their power lies ultimately in effective social ostracism, and not in the fines levied and the punishments decreed. Castes ban the intractable members and then expel any others who socialize with them. Villagers deny food, services, and fellowship to those who defy village decisions. Few can hold out against such an effective sanction. Most come to terms and plead for restoration of social roles and relationships. The cost of such settlements made by formal panchayats is considerable: there are fines, food for the elders during the session, and drinks to celebrate a successful settlement.

Caste panchayats are generally the final court of appeals in matters of caste customs. Some castes have regional panchayats ruling over specific territories. Others have caste gurus who pass judgment on caste affairs. Criminal and property cases, however, may be taken up by village panchayats if the caste fails to effect a settlement. Villages also deal with conflicts involving more than one caste. Failure to reach settlements at the village level generally leads to a feud or to its modern-day substitute, the state courts. Disgruntled losers may seek revenge in the courts where they do not expect to win as much as they want to harass their foes with high costs and time-consuming procedures. But men who go to court suffer the disapproval of the village and of its leaders, who stress the importance of village unity and harmony.

The ability of the indigenous panchayat system to reduce social tensions and to maintain social communication is evident from the low number of cases filed in the state courts from the plateau. Konduru Circle includes over twenty-five thousand people living in more than thirty villages and hamlets, yet according to the *munsif* judge of the taluk court with jurisdiction over the area, only twenty-three civil and nineteen criminal cases were filed from the area in 1964 (see Table 14).* He noted further that many of the civil cases were filed by both parties in collusion to circumvent state laws forbidding the sale of lands under certain circumstances. When the *tasildars* were empowered to handle land sales, the number of civil cases filed in the taluk court fell to three in 1965. In the same year only twenty criminal cases were filed from the Konduru Circle.

Table 14. Court Cases from the Konduru Circle Filed in the Nagerkurnool Munsif Court during 1964 and 1965

Type of Case	Number of Cases Filed in 1964	Number of Cases Filed in 1965
Civil cases........................	23	3
Criminal cases		
Criminal trespass	0	1
Injury and beatings..............	4	2
Theft	6	5
House trespass...................	2	2
Wrongful restraint................	2	1
Assault without injury............	3	3
Outraging the modesty of a woman...	1	0
Unlawful making of explosives......	1	0
Murder	0	1
Mischief with loss or damage.......	0	1
Adultery	0	1
Mischief by fire..................	0	1
Restraining public servants from doing their duty.................	0	1
Total number of criminal cases.....	19	20
Total number of all cases...........	42	23

The procedures and powers of panchayat are best studied by using the trouble-case method developed by Hoebel and Llewellyn (Llewellyn and Hoebel, 1941). Although procedures vary depending upon the

* Konduru's Gram Panchayat had no official judicial powers as of 1965. On occasion, it informally discussed current disputes, but passed no judgment upon them except to let the current consensus influence Panchayat decisions involving the parties, e.g. in the granting of loans, etc. The *tasildar* with jurisdiction over the area did, however, judge petty cases and was able to settle many of them. Hence, the figures in Table 14 do not reflect the total number of cases that were actually taken above the indigenous panchayat system to the formal government structures for settlement.

nature of the case and the contestants involved, clear patterns do emerge which point out the principles underlying the panchayat system.

Conflicts between men of the same caste and village frequently deal with inheritance and social relationships. Out of fifteen cases* within the same caste and village on the plateau, which occurred between 1946 and 1965, three dealt with the division of inherited lands, one with leadership rivalry, one with slander, and ten with family problems. Of the ten, four were cases of adultery, two of jealousy, two of cruelty, and one each of divorce and desertion. Problems relating to divorce and desertion are more common than these figures would indicate, since most marriages involve persons from different villages.

"Dividing an inheritance is always a problem," said Merchant Ramayya one day. When his own father died, his two brothers asked him to divide the inheritance although he was second in succession. The youngest chose his share first, the eldest selected next, and the remainder fell to Ramayya since he had been responsible for the arrangements. Walls were built dividing the large shop and house of their father. Ramayya was left the narrow central hall wedged between the two corner shops; but even so his brothers were jealous.

Not all divisions are just, and a disgruntled younger brother often tries to possess what he feels is his share.

&& Surayya, a Kappu farmer of Kodonpalli,† had argued for months with his older brother Kortayya, and had finally gone to the elders to get what he felt was his fair share of the inheritance, but all efforts failed. If anything were to come of his dissatisfaction, he would have to act on his own; one night he dug up the boundary rocks marking the corners of the fields and moved them a few feet. Kortayya noticed on the next day what had been done and confronted his brother, who proceeded to deny the whole affair. Then Kortayya went to Ramalingam, the village *sarpanch*, who, after investigating the matter with the elders, ordered Surayya to move the rocks back.

Having lost face and his claims to the land, Surayya struck back at Ramalingam whom he blamed for his humiliation. Supported by other

---

* These are the cases recorded by the author.
† Kodonpalli is a hamlet of Podur.

malcontented young men he sought to oust Ramalingam from office by charges of incompetency. He gave one hundred rupees to two constables for their support when they came to investigate Ramalingam's complaint of harassment. Three days later he added another hundred after the constables returned saying the other constables at headquarters had to be persuaded as well. When finally a hearing was held at the police office, Surayya stood no chance, for the subinspector of police was a friend of Ramalingam. Reprimanded by the officer, Surayya lost his temper and demanded his money back. The subinspector, hearing of the bribes, threatened to file criminal charges if three hundred rupees were not forthcoming, and Surayya, having no other place to turn, sold two cows and gave the inspector the money.ᛞᛞ

Several patterns emerge from this case. Individuals seeking redress often resort to intrigue or force. So long as the dispute remains in the argument stage the defending party gains by maintaining the status quo. Some move must be made to force the issue. Surayya chose to move the boundary stones, and, by so doing, to place the burden of action upon his brother. Then Kortayya was forced to put the stones back and face a fight or appeal to the village leaders, which he did. Had he kept quiet or vacillated, Surayya would have won his point.

The role of alliances is also clear in this situation. Personal disputes seldom remain such since participants seek supporters to strengthen their cases. The problem of the inheritance was lost when old grievances were resurrected and new ones created. Each party attacked the other at any vulnerable point, and, in turn, had to guard against attacks from any quarter. In this instance, the role of the village police was that of a neutral party seeking to gain personal advantages by playing the combatants off against each other. The lowest-ranking constables took gifts in exchange for promises of support. Even though they had no power of decision, Surayya knew that without their aid he had little hope for a favorable settlement. The subinspector, on the other hand, has the power to file criminal charges or to withhold them. In the end neither the subinspector nor Surayya wanted to face a prolonged court case. To save face, however, a few were willing to incur the disapproval of the villagers and the costs of a law case which could greatly exceed the value of the property under dispute.

This was the feeling Rangayya had in an incident with Barber Lingayya.

ↄↄ In 1946 Barber Lingayya found the opportunity he had been looking for to claim some lands which he felt were his share of the inheritance from his brother Rangayya. When the Muslim who had rented one of Rangayya's fields left town, Lingayya plowed and seeded it before Rangayya knew anything about it. Rangayya complained to his caste elders, but they knew that he had, indeed, been unfair in dividing the inheritance and told him to keep quiet. Finding no support in the village, Rangayya turned to the courts for redress. Here too he lost, although he appealed all the way to the district court. Twenty years have passed, but Rangayya has not yet settled his differences with his brother. ↄↄ

Social disputes frequently center around the marital tie. Divorce as a solution is forbidden by the high castes but is practiced by the low castes and Muslims. Causes for divorce include mental retardation of a spouse married in childhood, infertility on the part of the wife, abandonment, or adultery. A divorce is often arranged by mutual agreement; from each party the elders take signed statements releasing the other from future claims. If both parties do not agree, the settlement may be more difficult, as it was with one case which the Washerman headman told me about in 1964.

ↄↄ "A few months ago we went to settle a case in Podur. Pullayya had gone to Rameshvaram to get his wife who was visiting her parents, but she refused to return home with him. 'I won't have you as a husband,' she said. 'You are deformed, and besides that you are younger than I.' She could not be persuaded, even by the local elders, so Pullayya came to me and I arranged for a panchayat. Even after we urged her to return, she would not go. Finally, we ordered her parents to pay the husband three hundred rupees to cover his wedding expenses. They brought two hundred pleading, 'We are poor folk and cannot pay more than this.' We accepted the amount and divided up the household articles. The large pot and two small vessels that the wife had brought to the home were returned to her, together with a large brass plate. She had to return the gold earrings, hair clips, and bracelets her husband had given to her. We gave him one hundred fifty rupees of the money and used the rest to buy liquor to celebrate the settlement. Both are now remarried. The woman's second husband had to pay her parents the two hundred rupees they had spent for the divorce." ᛋᛋ

The ritual drink at the end of a case is characteristic of many successful panchayats. Both parties concerned in the controversy join the elders and onlookers in showing their acceptance of the decisions and the restoration of goodwill. There may be others besides the quarreling spouses who must also be placated, namely, kinsmen. The Leatherworker headman was aware of this when he settled the case involving an incensed mother-in-law in 1964.

ᛋᛋLittle Bukayya beat his wife with a stick one evening when the evening meal was not ready. This performance was not unusual, but Bukayya's mother-in-law was present. Hearing the cries of her daughter, she came to shield her from the blows. But Bukayya would not stop — in his anger he committed the unpardonable sin of striking his mother-in-law. The old woman began to cry, 'Ayyo, this is a barbaric place! These forest people are uncivilized.' The elders, relaxing before their evening meals, came running. Having heard her story, they tried to assure her that theirs was a respectable village. They promised they would meet the next day and punish the man.

Before dawn the next morning the mother-in-law set out for the nearby hamlet of Chintalonpalli to go to the home of the Pedda Maitry, regional headman of the plateau Leatherworkers, and pour out her woes. The panchayat was in session when the two returned. Time had cooled the husband's temper and he was ready now to set matters straight. The elders knew that he was a good man, not habitually in trouble, but that he had something of a temper. However, the mother-in-law's honor had to be satisfied and the village reputation preserved. After much discussion, they fined Bukayya sixty rupees and ordered him to apologize to his mother-in-law publicly. Knowing that she was not fully satisfied with the verdict, they assured her that this was his first offense and that they would surely outcaste him if he were to repeat the crime. Later on Bukayya returned; he had managed to beg and borrow twenty-five rupees which he offered as a token of his sincerity and pleaded poverty. The mother-in-law, in the meantime, had gone home so the elders granted his plea and bought drinks all around with the money. ᛋᛋ

In many cases the public harangues and heavy fines are aimed at placating offended parties and satisfying an interested audience. When the actual payment is made, smaller sums are generally accepted as an acknowledgment of guilt and subordination to the caste. The aim of the panchayat is not so much to punish an offender for a legal infraction, though this aspect cannot be ignored, as it is to seek a workable resolution of the crisis and a restoration of all members back into the caste fold. The verdict emphasizes the corporate power of the caste as caste, particularly when all of the fine goes to the elders and their drinking associates and none to the injured party, as was true in the situation just cited.

Slander is another occasion for a panchayat. "A man who is slandered cannot keep quiet. If he does, everyone will believe the charges were true and will ridicule him. Moreover the elders will be angry with him for not defending himself," said Devapriyam as he explained the experience of his friend, the Leatherworker.

ᛠᛠ"One hot day two young men of our hamlet began to quarrel. Balayya called Papayya a 'bastard.' Papayya could not let the matter drop or everyone would think the charge was true. With the help of his friends he caught the slanderer and dragged him to the public square. The friends tied Balayya's leg to Papayya's leg and both sat in the hot sun until some elders gathered to settle the argument. The two men were then untied and seated apart from the elders. Both would be thought of as guilty until the panchayat decided who was at fault. After listening to the stories, the elders ordered Balayya to prove his charge. How could he? He could not point out the real father without slandering another man, even though the matter was common gossip. No man would ever admit to the charges. So Balayya had to pay a fine which was used to buy palm beer."ᛠᛠ

In panchayats both parties concerned in the altercation are considered guilty of violating the peace and under caste suspension until judgment is passed. They are seated apart from those gathered to discuss the case and no one may socialize with them while the trial is pending. Only after a settlement has been reached are the parties seated at the end of the row of elders and given a share in the libations of reincorporation. If the panchayat fails, no one drinks.

Justice meted out by a panchayat is not based on the narrow technical issues of the case. There are no inflexible standards of right and wrong that must be enforced at all costs. The elders have known the disputants for years and are aware of the relationships between them; they also realize that both parties must continue to live together in the same village in the future. A poor settlement only breeds more trouble; but a good one repairs the rent seams of the social fabric. Panchayat settlements are the art of the socially possible. An excellent illustration of this is a settlement that caste headman Lakshayya effected and related to me in 1964.

&& "One of our local bachelors got into trouble with the wife of another Washerman named Chendrayya. It was common knowledge, but no one, not even his friends, would tell Chendrayya; they did not want to get into trouble or make him feel bad. Chendrayya suspected something. He tried beating his wife; but she denied everything. Finally, one day Chendrayya left as though he were going to work but turned the corner and hid behind a mud wall. When he saw the bachelor sneak into his house, he crept up to the house and snapped a big lock on the door [like most houses this one had no windows or back door]. Then he went to call the police. They were only too willing to arrest the culprits and lock them up in jail. When I heard about this affair, I said to myself that nothing good would come of it if the case went to court. I went to Krishna Chari and told him we should settle the matter within the village. He agreed and gave me a note for the patwari. The patwari and I went to see the police. They agreed to release the couple to us for seventy rupees which I paid.

"Since the matter was serious, I locked the couple up in my house. I needed the support of my caste and the village so I called in more than forty men from many castes. Elders from the Barber, Muslim, and Harijan castes were also present. The problem was a difficult one. The guilty coupled loved each other. On the other hand, the wife had several children including an infant boy two months old, and the bachelor was too poor to support a wife. If we granted a divorce, the husband would take the children, a solution that would be hard for the unweaned infant. We decided that for the children's sake the husband and wife should remain together. The husband was the key to the problem. He was proud and did not want his wife back. If we could first persuade him, the rest would be easy. I bought drinks around and we went to the husband's house. We asked him what had happened. He said, 'My wife slept with another man.' 'Did you have any proof?' we asked. 'I caught them both in my house and called the police,' he replied. As soon as he admitted calling the police, we found fault with him. He had insulted the caste by ignoring the elders and going directly to the police. Moreover, he had charged an innocent woman without witnesses. We knew the wife was guilty, but we did not dare admit it. We fined the man five hundred rupees for dishonoring the caste. By now he was quite humble and ready to take his wife back, and we agreed to drop the fine if he did so.

"Next we dealt with the woman. To make certain that the trouble would not be repeated, we made her sign a paper that if she were caught with the bachelor again she would have to pay the caste five hundred rupees. Finally we got to the bachelor who was the cause of the trouble. We fined him one hundred fifty rupees and made him sign a bond as well. I took seventy rupees to repay what I had given to the police, and the rest we used for celebrations." ʊ ʊ

While a man's status plays an important part in panchayat proceedings against him, not even a caste headman is above accusation and punishment. The headman is the de jure head by reason of his birth in the senior lineage of the caste. He must be given first honors at caste rituals, and his place must be acknowledged in the panchayats. He is the de facto leader only as long as he is able to prove his ability in maintaining discipline and justice for all within the caste community including himself. If he fails in this, other elders may usurp his authority, though not his office. One leading Weaver said of Big Ballayya, his caste headman, "He is a good leader. He does not try to hide it when he gets into trouble himself." In 1965, he was discussing the current case of a negligent headman.

ʊ ʊ Big Balayya was responsible for guarding his widowed daughter from immorality after she returned home because her husband had left her no inheritance. When he found out that his daughter was pregnant, he knew that he would have to act, for the elders would eventually find out about the affair. He called the caste leaders together and explained the facts. They fined him for negligence and were investigating further when the frightened adulterer appeared, offering to pay to keep the matter quiet. The elders decided that there was no use in forcing another wife and child on a man who already had difficulty supporting his own family. On the other hand, the expected child needed a legal father to give it lineage and caste ties, for no man would marry his offspring to a person without these. The elders let the adulterer off with a fine and ordered Big Balayya to find his daughter a husband before the child was born.

After a long search, the parents found an old Weaver of seventy whose cantankerous wife had died years before. He was now content to live alone. When they first approached him, he was not interested. Even after they promised to pay all costs including the wedding, the fifty rupee fine he would have to pay the caste for marrying an adulteress, and the support of the woman and child for life, he still was not interested. Finally the headman appealed to the elders and they, too, pressured the old man to help the child by going through with the marriage. They assured him that he would not have to live with the woman if he did not want to. In the end the old man consented. A "sari-jacket" (*shira rike*) marriage was arranged; it was the second marriage for both of them and tainted besides. The old man gave the bride a sari and a jacket. There was no feast nor any exchange of gifts. The baby girl who was born shortly thereafter was given the house and lineage names of the old man and she is now an accepted member of the caste. Depending upon the social climate at the time, the couple sometimes lives together and sometimes apart. ৬৬

The caste headman could not hide the facts of the case. He could have withstood challenges to his leadership, but he knew that public opinion would be against him and this situation would weaken his position. By raising the issue himself, he forestalled criticism. In the end the settlement cost him a lot of money and he had to find a legal father so that the child would receive its properly ascribed status in society; however, the settlement also won him the respect of his fellow castemen.

In meting out punishment, elders take into account the social and economic status of the offender. The rich must pay well to satisfy the people; yet care must be taken in judging the powerful. Leniency is generally shown to those who submit to the caste and plead for mercy. In most observed cases even a partial payment of the fine was accepted as a token of submission and good faith. But the elders must resort to other forms of punishment, like a ceremony of ridicule, if the culprit is unable to pay even a small fine. This was the case with the pauper Pentayya.

❧❧Pentayya was drunk the night he beat his wife unmercifully. When the Leatherworker elders rebuked him, he ridiculed them in his stupor and dared them to stop him. The insulted elders met and fined him twenty-five rupees. The next day, sober and penitent, Pentayya pleaded destitution. All knew that he had absolutely nothing; hence, they demanded that he humble himself before them in lieu of the fine. While the men of the caste sat in a circle around a fire that night, Pentayya had to take off his lower dress. Squatting on the ground, he was ordered to pull himself back and forth across the ground on his buttocks while the onlookers poked fun at him. After all were satisfied, the man was let off. ❧❧

Only those with no other recourse consent to such humiliation. Moreover the elders let only the truly destitute get off in this manner. Villagers tell of a prosperous man in the past who, through miserliness, agreed to humble himself before the elders rather than pay a fine, only to find in the end that the elders imposed an even greater fine upon him for humiliating the whole caste before the village.

REGIONAL CASTE ORGANIZATIONS

Some more populous castes have regional caste organizations that have jurisdiction over a number of villages. The Washerman region of which Konduru is a part includes more than forty villages on the plateau and adjacent plains. Among the caste headmen of these villages, those from Konduru, Rameshvaram, Maradpur, and two plains villages are the regional leaders and Lakshayya of Konduru is their superior. As regional headman he is informed concerning general caste affairs and considers cases not solved on the village level. The Leatherworkers and Weavers have similar organizations covering the plateau. The former caste has four regional leaders headed by the Pedda Maitri who lives near Konduru. At all important caste functions these four must be acknowledged in their rank order. Their names are announced and, if food is served, they are given the first portions. In their absence, small spots of colored powder are made on some convenient post or pot to represent them. These spots are then addressed and served food as though they were the leaders. Only then can the formal ceremonies or the meetings proceed.

Regional problems include disagreements concerning caste customs and work monopolies, but a large share relate to social relationships such as marriage. Arguments may arise early in making marriage arrangements. Suitable gifts must be exchanged throughout the engagement period and stinginess is interpreted as an affront to the family. As the final terms of marriage are arranged each side evaluates closely the gifts or dowry that the other family offers. Guests may wait while the last differences are being settled. If the marriage is called off, who is to pay for the uneaten wedding feast? And how can one accept the insult of a canceled marriage? Crippled Yellayya, the Barber, sat on the palm-leaf mat as he told how he had helped to cut the Gordian knot for the Winetappers. Usually his lame leg is a curse to him, but this time it was an asset since people suspect crippled men, particularly Barbers, of being magicians. So when a marriage had to be rescheduled, Yellayya was called upon to help make sure that the ceremony actually would take place.

๕ ๕Wedding guests were gathering in Konduru and the feast was being prepared when a messenger arrived. The marriage was off! A cow had died the previous night at the home of the bride, which was considered a bad omen. The bridal party would not appear. The Winetapper and his wife could only wring their hands. For years they had exchanged gifts with the bride's parents. On their journeys to visit them they had been watching for other bad omens such as the sight of a broken pot or a corpse, but there were none. A Brahman had checked the horoscopes and chosen an auspicious moment for the wedding. All their efforts were to no avail. The messenger offered to return the twenty-five rupees and *vali* gifts, which the groom's parents had sent to the bride's mother to seal the arrangement, but the parents would not take them back. They were not giving up so easily.

Yellayya the Barber heard about the affair the next day as he was shaving one of the Winetappers. In half jest he said, "If such a thing happened to me, I would go and camp on their door steps, not letting anyone pass or cook meals, until they had given their daughter to me!" Word of his boasting reached the distraught parents who besought him to accompany a delegation going to fetch the girl. He could not turn back now. The girl's representative had stayed around, hoping to make peace, but when he heard that the crippled Barber was coming to his village, he hurried off to warn his kin.

Besides the Barber and the groom's older brother, the delegation included the groom's paternal uncle and his wife, who was a sister to the bride's mother and who had arranged the marriage in the first place. Fearing her sister's wrath, the woman absconded outside the village, and as the party wound down the ghat (mountain) road leading to the plains, the uncle decamped. The brother was ready to turn back but the Barber refused, for he did not want to be ridiculed as a coward who had gone along only for the food. When the two arrived at the village, they were received with the respect born from a fear of the Barber's magical powers. They were given food and water, but they could not get a commitment for the girl's hand in marriage. Finally, it was agreed that the case should go to the caste elders. Night had fallen by the time the elders gathered; drink flowed freely and tempers were unrestrained. When the headman asked Yellayya to speak, the Barber, who had kept himself sober, asked, "Do you want justice or passion?" The headman understood the inference and dismissed the case until the morning when all would be sober.

The following day the Barber, acting as spokesman for the groom, said that the parents would like to go through with the marriage. However, they were ready to forget the four hundred rupees lost in the ruined feast and to close the case as soon as the bride's party returned the *vali* and the cash equivalent for the many gifts that they had received over the years. The girl's mother was ready to return the money when some of her kinsmen warned her that the Barber wanted the money to file a court case against her. Although the Barber had no such plan, the mother was afraid. Seeing no other way out and realizing that public support backed the Barber, she reluctantly agreed to give her daughter at some future date.

Arrangements were made again, and another day set. Fearing further trouble, the groom's parents asked Yellayya to go along with the party sent to fetch the girl. Their fears were not unfounded — the mother had hidden the girl. The arguments ran long and loud. Other villagers joined in the altercation, and ridiculed the mother for her false promises. Finally the controversy was taken to the village patwari whose support the mother had obtained before the party arrived. To everyone's surprise the Barber turned out to be an old schoolmate of the patwari. After some reminiscing the Barber explained his case. The mother, seeing her only support vanish, yielded to public pressures and gave her daughter in marriage. ـʊـʊ

As is evident in this case, public sentiment is often an important factor in panchayat decisions. Meetings are often held in the open and an interested audience soon forms. Even if the onlookers do not participate in the formal proceedings, they serve as a sounding board for the feelings of the community.

Regional caste organizations maintain order within their territories. There is, however, no clear pattern for the settlement of disputes between men from different regions. A regional headman informs those of neighboring territories regarding caste decisions in his own area, but he cannot demand their enforcement elsewhere. The difficulties involved in maintaining relationships beyond the regional boundaries are obvious in the situation where a man agreed to marry his son to two women, one from his hometown and one from another town.

ـʊـʊGafoor of Konduru contracted to marry his daughter to the son of Abdul Khan of Podur. Gifts and messages were exchanged periodically, but suddenly communications ceased. The puzzled father went to investigate, and, to his distress, learned that Abdul had secretly arranged to marry his son to a girl from Ravila on the plains. Gafoor took his case to Muhammed Salim, head of the plateau Fakirs, who called a panchayat. The local caste body found Abdul guilty of breach of promise and ordered him to marry his son to Gafoor's daughter. Not daring to risk the ire of his caste, Abdul agreed and the marriage was performed. The people at Ravila heard of the wedding and sent a delegation of elders to demand their rights. The Konduru elders explained their decision to the men of Ravila who had no choice but to accept it. They had no means of enforcing their own claims since there was no common caste leadership to which they could appeal. ـʊـʊ

Abdul failed in his attempt to break his original contract by letting it lapse and presenting Gafoor with a fait accompli. Caught in his own intrigues, he had no recourse but to obey his own leaders and bear the insults of the people from Ravila. They, for their part, had no way to demand restitution for monies lost since they belonged to another caste region.

Castemen within a region often share a sense of loyalty to one another. In their quarrels with outsiders, people can usually count on the support of their own leaders. In 1965, headman Lakshayya told me about a case based on this principle.

ᘓᘓ"Some years ago we gave one of our women to a Washerman in Nagerkurnool, forty miles away. He mistreated her and would not listen to her parents' entreaties nor to us. This year when she came to visit her parents during the festival, she declared that she would not return with her husband when he came for her. The parents called us and we discussed the situation. The man was proud and would not listen to us because we were not his elders; consequently, we quietly married the woman to another man from our own area. The first husband was very angry when he found his wife married to another man. He went to call his elders from Nagerkurnool. We all sat together, and the men from Nagerkurnool soon realized that they could not do anything because we were united. We all agreed that the second husband should give the first husband two hundred fifty rupees. From this money we used thirty rupees to buy drinks to settle the matter. When there is unity, the people can do anything."ᘓᘓ

The elders from Nagerkurnool probably thought the abduction was a family plot and hoped to persuade the Konduru elders that their case was just. When they saw that it was the leaders who had instigated the action, they could only hope to act as mediators in claiming damages. Having won their point, the Konduru men wanted to close the case with the customary compensation. To have refused this payment could have only bred territorial feuds. Workable solutions such as this cannot always be reached, even with the aid of the village headman. Lakshayya reported the case involving his nephew's second marriage which was brought to court before it could be settled.

ᘓᘓ"My nephew, Somayya, married a local girl when both were very young. Later the girl turned out to be mentally retarded; so he arranged with the elders to pay her one hundred rupees and sent her home. At his age it was hard for the young man to find a wife. Eventually he heard of a young woman at Nagerkurnool who had been abandoned by her husband who had become a mendicant. Since the husband had not been heard of for three years, her parents consented to her marriage with Somayya. A year later the first husband showed up and demanded his wife back, but she refused to live with him. Even the Konduru Washermen elders could not convince him to take the three hundred rupees which the second husband offered in settlement. He brought the Nagerkurnool elders and we all discussed the case. The men of Nagerkurnool acknowledged the justice of our claims and tried to persuade their man to accept a settlement, but he would agree to no less than five hundred rupees. We could not reach an agreement; therefore, we took the case to Krishna Chari who suggested a compromise of three hundred fifty rupees. The disgruntled husband would not bargain and the panchayat broke up.

When the first husband filed a court case against the second in Nagerkurnool, we hired a lawyer for eighty rupees. After several months the case appeared to be going against the first husband, and rather than lose face he agreed to settle out of court for three hundred fifty rupees. If the man had listened to the elders there would not have been so much trouble or expense." ᛭ ᛭

Regional caste organizations maintain order within defined territories. Between regions there is no structure for settling differences, only a recourse to public pressures, ridicule, and the threat of feud. People form most ties within their own regions where they have the means to claim their rights, but connections may also be made with other regions to which people are linked by existing relationships and thus have avenues for applying pressure, if necessary. It is among the small castes with no territorial organizations that the average distance of marriage ties is great.

INTERCASTE CONFLICTS

The distinction between caste and village panchayats is not sharp. The difference does not lie in the composition of members involved in the discussions. While caste panchayats may be limited to men of a single caste, men from outside castes are commonly involved in a caste panchayat, particularly on matters concerning caste customs. Generally speaking, the difference lies in the leadership of the panchayat. In caste panchayats caste leaders preside, and in village panchayats the village headman and village officials take charge.

Village panchayats frequently deal with conflicts arising between castes. For instance, a caste can punish adultery if both parties are in its own ranks, but the problem is far more complex if the offenders come from different castes, as was the situation with Venkayya, his wife, and his wife's lover, the Muslim Yakobali.

↺↺Venkayya appealed to his Herdsmen elders when he could not stop an affair between his wife and the Muslim Yakobali. Because the case involved another caste the elders summoned Krishna Chari, the village patwari and the police patel. Yakobali denied seducing the woman. "What can I do? She comes of her own accord," he told them. When questioned the woman openly declared her love for Yakobali and her desire to be with him. Krishna Chari rebuked her for rejecting her caste duties, but she remained adamant. Yakobali agreed to take her into his house and the Herdsmen banned her from their caste. Because the arrangement was irregular, the village elders did not levy damages against Yakobali, but privately they told him to settle with the first husband. Yakobali sent some money to Venkayya by the hand of a mediator. The Herdsmen, for their part, lamented their weakness. One of them declared that if they had been strong and united as they had been in the past, they would have beaten the Muslim and guarded the woman against further troubles. ↺ ↺

The inaction of the Herdsmen is an indication of the effect power has on the panchayat's judgment. The Herdsmen are wealthy but are no match for the more numerous Muslims; hence, they do not dare to force the issue. Similarly a single man without the power base of fellow castemen to support him stands little chance against an entrenched group. This was the experience of Kama Kortayya, a prosperous farmer who came to farm in Konduru in 1963. The Kamas, whose strength lies south and east of the plateau, are rivals to the Reddis who occupy Telengana and overflow onto the plateau. Even so, Kortayya might have succeeded if it weren't for his constant boasting about the superior farming abilities of the Kamas, which infuriated the local Reddis and incurred the ire of Konduru's leaders.

↺↺The Muslim Ikbal Gafoor sold Kama Kortayya the tract of land within the crumbling walls of the former village fort. After Kortayya had farmed the soil for several years, Gafoor wanted it back, and insisted that he had only rented it. Many villagers said some of the village leaders did not want Kortayya around and instigated Gafoor's actions. The only official land records of the village, kept by the patwari, showed no record of the sale. Kortayya had planted his crops so he asked for time to reap the harvest, but Gafoor refused this request. One night the crops were cut to the ground. In desperation, Kortayya asked Gafoor for the money he had originally paid for the land and Gafoor returned eight hundred rupees. Since he was the only Kama in town, Kortayya had no place to turn for support. Many villagers felt sorry for him and said he had been treated unjustly, but the village leaders lined up behind Gafoor against this outsider who listened to the complaints of the poor and told the rest how to farm. So matters stood until Kahrim returned.

The eldest son Kahrim was considered to be the black sheep of Gafoor's parental home since he rebelled and left the village for government service. His father had disinherited him, and the family land went to Gafoor. Upon returning, Kahrim saw an opportunity to claim part of his deceased father's land. Making friends with Kortayya, he incited the Kama to use the eight hundred rupees to file a legal case against Gafoor and the patwari. Kortayya's case became a cause célèbre for the village. After the sudden death of the rightful patwari a few years back, the office was given temporarily to a distant relative until the heirs came of age. The new patwari had the reputation among many of being a hard man. Villagers noted in private that although he was poor when he came, within a few years he built a new rock mansion. Dissatisfaction split the village; some supported the patwari, but others secretly sided with Kortayya.

Villagers still tell of the District Collector's visit to Konduru to investigate the charges filed by Kortayya and some villagers who claimed that the patwari had not returned to them tax monies refunded by the government when the peanut crop failed. Finding the records not in order, the Collector suspended the patwari and appointed another man in his place. He did not review the land case because it was in court. But if Kortayya had gained the backing of the Collector and many common folk, he had also incurred the undying enmity of the patwari for instigating his suspension. When the Collector left, Kortayya's power left with him. The villagers did not dare oppose the village leadership openly; thus, Kortayya was left alone. He stayed in

Konduru for another year, while the case was being shunted between low and high courts. For a time he clung to the hope that the land would eventually be his, but in the end he came to realize that even if he had it, he could not stay on alone in an alien village. ↶↶

There are many reasons why Kortayya failed. He was an outsider and a braggart. He allied himself with the poor villagers and posed a threat to the authority of the village leaders. Finally, he had no kin, castemen, or patron to support him when the case came to a show-down. The legal sanctions against the patwari, on the other hand, were easily circumvented, for the newly appointed patwari was content to be a figurehead. Claiming ignorance of land matters, he simply left the books at the home of the old patwari and signed the documents as he was told.

Village panchayats are important in maintaining village life. They serve as courts of appeal for caste decisions and bridge the cleavages dividing castes and communities. Their strength lies in their ability to enlist public support and engender village unity. Old men filled with nostalgia idealize the days when a village acted as a whole, when its leaders could ban rebels from its territories, and when the villagers joined together to cut off social and economic ties with renegades. But in reality fission and rivalry have always been a threat to village harmony. Today the inroads of the outside world are further undermining the traditional village power structures. Even so, the ideal of village harmony and the panchayat system as a means to pursue this ideal remain important factors in the stability of village life.

INTERVILLAGE CONFLICTS

The village acts as a unit in relation to the external world of other villages. Although villagers are commonly in competition with each other, when external threats appear, these rivalries are usually forgotten. Villagers unite to present a common front, if only because they must live together the next day. Their only support may be silence when to speak would endanger a fellow man, but as I noted during an incident that occurred while accompanying a group of elders to another village, even this silence can be most effective.

↶↶Four Weaver elders knocked on my door with a request for me to accompany them to Kalampalli beneath the escarpment on the plains.

What they really needed was my jeep. I agreed to go because I wanted to observe the settlement of a case of elopement. On the road the outlines of the case became clear. The daughter of one of the men had eloped with a Muslim truck driver and was living in Kalampalli with his first wife. She was now working there in the maternity center. Strategy was discussed. Should we sneak up on the village and capture the girl? Should we call in the police and have her arrested? In the end, caution carried the day, and we stopped at Maredpur to consult with the regional health administrator in charge of the runaway girl. This woman offered to go in her jeep first to see if she could persuade the girl to return. The suggestion was accepted and we set up camp under the shade of a tree at the base of the escarpment. Mealtime came and went, but the woman did not return. Finally, four hours later, she arrived, minus the girl. No persuasion or threats to withhold wages had changed the girl's mind.

What were we to do next? Another council was called and all agreed that we should storm the village. On the road we passed the Kalampalli police patel and took him aboard. He agreed to help. The jeep had barely stopped when the elders and the patel set out to catch the girl, but she was not to be found. We asked every bystander but no one had the slightest idea of her whereabouts. "She was here a half hour ago. She must have run off into the fields with the truck driver," was the standard answer. Not even the man's wife knew where her husband and his lover were. The policeman harangued his villagers, and the houses were ransacked, but it was no use, the couple had disappeared.

On the road home, the elders argued over their failure. The administrator had, no doubt, given them away. Some thought they should have sneaked up without warning, while others argued that they should have gone at night. But all agreed that the basic problem was the lack of Weavers living in the town to whom they could appeal for help. The discussion switched to consideration of further action. One suggestion was that they hide for a time and return suddenly; another was that they come secretly at night with an oxcart and police. But most of the elders were tired of the case. They had missed their noon meal and some had hired help sitting idly in the fields. After the distraught father bought them meals at a roadside restaurant they returned home empty-handed. ᰆᰆ

It was clear that some of the villagers knew the hiding place of the elopers. They did not condone the couple's action; yet the man was of their own village and even the Konduru elders admitted that his own people must support him. When conflicts involve whole villages, a sense of loyalty to the hometown is of particular importance. Some villages, such as Danvada on the nearby plains, are known for their esprit de corps. When Danvada's struggle with the adjacent village of Mandodi came to blows over a desecrated bull, in 1958, men beat their fellow castemen and kinsmen while upholding the honor of their own village.

↳↳ Peddamma, the village goddess of Danvada, resides in a small cairn beside the road. In the village, the elders decided that she should be propitiated so that the village would gain prosperity and strength. A young buffalo bull was dedicated to her and released for several months to fatten up. Such a bull, untied and untamed, is permitted to roam freely over the countryside. Those in whose fields it feeds are blessed.

One day the bull turned up at nearby Mandodi. There it got into trouble when it charged a woman and gored her with its horns. The villagers knew that it was dedicated to the gods because it had a large iron ring around one of the forelegs; however, they were angry. This was not the first time the bull had caused trouble. They beat the bull and locked it up in the village cow pound.

The men of Danvada heard of the incident and anticipated a fight. Their opportunity came when the Mandodi farmers set out for their fields the next morning. Each village has a well-defined boundary around the fields which are traditionally accepted as a part of the village. Danvada's territory is large and many men from Mandodi rent or own Danvada lands. When the farmers arrived at the boundary between the villages, they were confronted by over three hundred men from Danvada who confiscated their cattle and implements. In reply a large band of Mandodi men gathered to put Danvada in its place. The two armies met at the boundary; the men of Mandodi were beaten. Defiantly the Danvada men paraded across Mandodi lands.

Mandodi had more men than Danvada, but was split by factions to the point where no man trusted another in battle. The elders realized that they could not win a battle and that Mandodi stood to lose the most in a standoff because few Danvada men farmed Mandodi lands, so they agreed to write a letter of peace. In it they expressed willingness to acknowledge their guilt and to pay damages if a joint panchayat should find them at fault. The Danvada elders replied that they too wanted a peaceful settlement. Under the truce fifty Mandodi elders met in Danvada with thirty of its elders to settle the case. The young men of Danvada, hot tempered and heady with success, were not about to have their goddess insulted and their village compromised. While the elders sat debating, the young men caught three Mandodi negotiators and carried them off, despite the pleas of the Danvada leaders. The captives, fearing for their lives, made promises to meet any demands made upon them. Finally the youths returned their captives and announced the terms for settlement: the Mandodi people would have to buy a new bull to replace the desecrated one, and, in acknowledgment of their error, they should send twenty men to humble themselves before Peddamma when the new bull was sacrificed. Furthermore, the men of Mandodi should show respect to the men of Danvada in the future.

Back at Mandodi tempers flared. The young men wanted war, but the elders knew they only stood to lose even more in open battle. In the end moderation won out. A bull was purchased and escorted to the Danvada goddess by twenty men selected for their self-control lest any of them lose his temper and the feud be renewed. ༒ ༒

In the past petty kings and zamindars took cognizance of intervillage disputes. Today the state government may intervene. But the threat of feud often provides the most persuasive argument for a settlement between warring villages. While a face-saving compromise is generally sought, in the end power has a great deal of influence in determining the final terms.

KONDURU AND THE STATE GOVERNMENT

Konduru villagers frequently speak of the state and national government officials as though they are outsiders. They are aware (1) of the greater measure of safety provided by these governments, which was not available even a few decades ago when marauding bandits inhabited the nearby forests, (2) of the new schools and roads springing up everywhere, and (3) of new government services. They are also aware of revenue collectors, forest rangers, and policemen who tax them and regulate their behavior. In the past, authority radiated from the state government down to the district and taluk levels (see Figure 16). Officials toured the countryside inspecting programs and ordering changes. The chief contact the villager had with the outside world was through the local police and the patwari who was authorized by the state to keep land records and collect revenue. Some villagers had appeared before the *tasildar*, and a few had taken cases to the *munsif* court or to the district court.

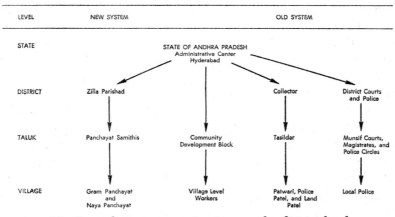

LEVEL	NEW SYSTEM			OLD SYSTEM	
STATE		STATE OF ANDHRA PRADESH Administrative Center Hyderabad			
DISTRICT	Zilla Parishad		Collector		District Courts and Police
TALUK	Panchayat Samithis	Community Development Block	Tasildar		Munsif Courts, Magistrates, and Police Circles
VILLAGE	Gram Panchayat and Naya Panchayat	Village Level Workers	Patwari, Police Patel, and Land Patel		Local Police

16. General government structure on the district level

In an attempt to involve the villagers in the government processes, the Government of India introduced a new form of government called Panchayati Raj based upon the principle of the democratic decentralization of power. The initial stage was introduced on the plateau in 1958 with the establishment of Gram Panchayats or elected village councils which were given such responsibilities as village sanitation, the planning and regulation of local markets, and the oversight of village development in general. Villagers elected *panches* to the council and these members in turn elected their own chairman called the *sarpanch*. The plateau was integrated into the second and third stages of Panchayati Raj in 1960. *Sarpanches* from the plateau joined those from the adjacent plains to form the regional Maradpur Panchayati Samiti. This Samiti coincided with the Tribal Development Block through which the Andhra Pradesh State Government sought to initiate economic and social progress on the plateau. In 1964 the Maradpur Tribal Block was merged with the Achampet Block to then form the Achampet Community Development Block directed by the Block Development Officer (B.D.O.). This officer works with the Achampet Samiti to initiate government programs such as cooperatives, agricultural extension, handicrafts, and elementary education. On the highest level the Samiti presidents within the district meet to form the Mahbubnagar Zilla Parishad which administers district projects.

The impact of the new structure is only beginning to be felt. Villagers sense the power of their vote in their local elections, even though they often elect their traditional leaders to office. Others find elections a new avenue through which they can gain status. No longer can a leader ignore the voices of the villagers, at least during election times. He must appeal to them through promises of aid and sometimes through threats. Politics opened up new avenues for the expression of caste and personal rivalries. But in matters of law and order the police and local officers still serve as the intermediaries between the people and the government. It is the forest officer who forbids their gathering of wood in the nearby forest reserve, the patwari who collects the taxes, and the police who investigate social irregularities. The latter, like the district attorney in the United States, by using their authority to file criminal suits or to withhold action, can often settle conflicts without ever going to court. A Konduru elder told me about such a case in which two thieves were accidentally poisoned.

ᘓᘓWinetapper Narayya could not catch the thieves who emptied some of his pots hanging from the palm trees. He had the government contract to tap the palm sap and brew the local beer. Finally he resorted to desperate measures: he baited some of his pots with poison, in an attempt to paralyze the freebooters. The trap was sprung, but instead of sick thieves, the Winetapper found the bodies of two young men. To cover up the crime he weighted the bodies and disposed of them in a nearby well.

Later the same day the parents, who were Leatherworkers and Weavers from a hamlet close by, came looking for their sons. They knew of their sons' escapades and suspected foul play, but when they accused the contractor of murder he denied everything. In despair they called the police. During the ensuing investigations one of the constables took the Winetapper aside and suggested the matter could be settled quietly. Narayya agreed and offered five hundred rupees if the case were closed. The parents publicly offered a reward of eight hundred if the bodies were found and the killer prosecuted, but they were poor and had no money in hand.

The case might have ended there, but just then a lad came running; one of the bodies had been seen floating in the well. The case went for further investigation to the subinspector of police who has the authority to file criminal proceedings. The Winetapper admitted his action and offered another three hundred rupees if charges were dropped. When the police officer talked to the parents, he told them that because their sons were committing a crime at the time criminal proceedings were not justified. He suggested they settle out of court, and when they would not agree he told them to file their own suit. They begged him to prosecute, but their request was continually delayed. The parents had no money to go to court, and they knew that they stood little chance without the support of the police even if they did. ↳↳

When such cases go unsettled, they breed distrust for formal law on the part of the villagers. So long as a semblance of justice and order is maintained, police are accepted as part of life. But when public opinion builds up, it can explode in a display of anger and violence. At such times the village closes ranks against the outside world. Following the case of the Gypsy's death (discussed in chapter five), village resentment smoldered over the believed injustice of the case. This resentment flared in the brief peasant's revolt twelve months later, in May 1965.

↳↳ The Muslim leaders took down the large man-shaped *pērlas* depicting great saints from the nets tied up against the ceilings of their houses and led religious processions down to the well to bathe them. The priestly Mullas arrived late and a husky, sharp-tongued Tanner chided them, "You're our rich priests, but you're more interested in your sleep and money than in serving God." The Mullas bore the chiding only so long, before they turned and beat the man. Hearing the noise, the police came running and took the Tanner into custody. On the way back to the police compound, the head constable swung his stick around to clear away the children crowding around. Suddenly a lad fell to the ground.

"He's dead!" The cry spread like wildfire as people recalled the death of the Gypsy a year earlier. The constable fled as the mob gathered, crying and milling around the police yard. The subinspector arrived with several constables and tried to calm the frenzy, but the burly Tanner grabbed him by the collar, set him down, and with the others made him sign a statement concerning the facts of the case as they dictated them to him. The boy, who was not dead but unconscious, was taken home. The officer agreed to call a meeting the next day, and gradually the crowd broke up.

The next morning, the thirteenth of May, everyone gathered for the meeting, only to find that they had been double-crossed. During the night the subinspector had sent a constable to summon the District Superintendent of Police. While the men were milling around, several jeep loads of police arrived, and a mass meeting was called. Eighty-five men were charged with rioting and damaging police property. Leading villagers were pressured into testifying against them, but in the turmoil no signed statements were recorded. After some delay criminal charges were filed in Nagerkurnool by the police against twenty-seven men, who had not paid to have their names struck from the list.

"There were eighteen witnesses," said Farmer Chendrayya, one of the defendants, "nine of them police. But because the judge did not depend upon the testimony of the police, the case rested on the witness of the nine villagers including Krishna Chari, Balayya, and others. We met with them and asked, 'Why do you want to testify against us? These police come and go, but we must live in the village together.' Because they had not signed written statements, they agreed to help us. When they gave their testimony, each said that he had heard the noise and knew there was trouble, but that he had not actually seen any of us doing anything wrong. One said he was at home; another that he was by the temple. We knew then that we would win." The case was dismissed on the twentieth of October. The defendants were acquitted. ઠઠ

Their success won the defendants prestige among the villagers and respect from the police — Konduru had its own John Hampdens. At the crucial moment, the village elders sided with their fellow men by presenting useless testimony, and sabotaged the police by turning their own game against them. Thus, village solidarity was reaffirmed.

Harmony and conflict are recurrent themes in the village. Students of the Konduru high school were asked to write brief stories about a picture in which several men were standing around talking. One of the men was gesturing to the others. Out of fifty-five stories, sixty-two percent described fights of which one-half were between brothers, and then usually over inheritance. In these the role of a mediator is almost invariably present in the form of a brother, father, friend, or village elder trying to make peace. Seven of the fights were settled by panchayats, three by courts, and four by kings. Six ended in stalemates and the balance left the settlement undetermined. Many of the stories closed with the moral, "In unity there is strength, in division is weakness," or "If they stand together, brothers can do anything."

PANCHAYATS AND COURTS

The British system of jurisprudence, which was introduced into India during the colonial era, imitated by the princely state of Hyderabad, and later incorporated into modern independent India, stands in sharp contrast to the systems of customary law that have been operating in Konduru. To the villager the former is foreign and, for the most part, incomprehensible. Those who turn to the police and courts are thought to flout the authority and solidarity of the village. Efforts to incorporate Hindu and Muslim law into the new legal system and to adapt it to village culture have failed to a considerable extent to turn the villagers to the police and courts for justice. To some extent this failure rests upon the fact that the Hindu and Muslim laws incorporated into the court system were taken largely from ancient orthodox codifications from high culture rather than from the current peasant law of the villages. As Rudolph points out (1967), Hindu codes of law which were formulated centuries ago for a small segment of society, the twice-born, were applied to the whole of Hindu society, and orthodox Islamic codes were imposed upon Muslim converts who had retained many of their Hindu ways. To a greater extent, however, the failure lay in the fundamental differences between the two systems of jurisprudence — differences apparent from Konduru's panchayat cases. To use Landis' terms (Unnithan 1965), the difference between the panchayats and the courts is the difference between therapeutic and punitive justice. While the aim of the latter is to punish injustice determined by a single universal standard of justice, the panchayat seeks to restore harmony by acknowledging the uniqueness of each situation, the differences between men, and the necessity for saving face. Panchayat is the art of the socially possible rather than the science of the morally right. This view of law has far-reaching consequences. The arbiters of a panchayat are those mutually involved with the outcome of the case, not detached dispassionate judges. The parties involved are both on trial and the case can swing against either, though usually a measure of compromise is involved. In the court based upon the adversary principle, one party is a plaintiff and the other a defendant. The settlement is clear cut, either win or lose or innocent or guilty. In panchayats witnesses are intimately known and are expected to support their kin and castemen while in the court witnesses are supposed to declare the impartial truth. Panchayats review the total social context, not a narrow point of law, and then frequently deal with some unsurfaced problem beneath the visible case at hand. Because decisions are enforced by social ostracism rather than active intervention, they are arrived at by community consensus rather than by a verdict reached by a few. I concur with Sriniva's position when he notes (Marriott 1955:18) that it is not that justice administered by the elders is "always or even usually more just than the justice administered by the judges in urban law courts, but only that it is better understood by the litigants."

One of the prerequisites for a stable society is an effective legal system; one which, as E. Adamson Hoebel points out (1954:275), fulfills the following functions:

The first is to define relationships among the members of a society, to assert what activities are permitted and what are ruled out, so as to maintain at least minimal integration between the activities of individuals and groups within the society.

The second is . . . the allocation of authority and the determination of who may exercise physical coercion as a socially recognized privilege-right, along with the selection of the most effective forms of physical sanction to achieve the social ends that the law serves.

The third is the disposition of trouble cases as they arise.

The fourth is to redefine relations between individuals and groups as the conditions of life change. It is to maintain adaptability.

The panchayat system operating within the framework of the caste structure does indeed fulfill these functions and, therefore, plays an important part in maintaining the stability of village life.

CHAPTER SEVEN

RITUALS

THE people of Konduru believe that the village is also inhabited by innumerable supernatural beings whose activities are intimately related to those of the men and beasts who live in the same village. Gods and demigods, spirits, ghosts, winds, powers, and such demonic beings as rākshasas, asuras, yakshas, and pisāchas are thought to inhabit almost every grove and field, well and house.

No sharp line divides natural beings from supernatural ones. Villagers vividly describe their encounters with ogres who have bulging eyes and shaggy hair and live in the bottoms of wells, or with demons who leap upon a man returning home in the black of night and pin him in his terror to the ground. Others have seen the beautiful seductresses whose love is intoxicating but fatal to the man who is led astray. There are the ghosts of the dead who have returned to find the fulfillment they were denied in life. There are capricious goddesses who decree life and prosperity or drought and destruction, according to their whims. There are also great gods who live in splendor in the heavens and who appear on earth in the temples where they can be seen by sincere devotees.

The lack of a sharp distinction between the natural and supernatural extends to explanations for the events of life. When Sayanna returned from the forest with a deep gash in his foot, he noted that the ax was dull; therefore, it had glanced off the hard wood of the tree. He added that the goddess Maicamma was angry with him because he had neglected to give her the traditional annual offering and, consequently, had caused the accident to punish him for his carelessness. Sayanna was aware of the natural causes that were responsible for his mishap, which answered the question about how it took place; however, for the why of the event, he accepted a supernatural explanation.

The distinctions between supernatural and natural and between sacred and secular are useful so long as one realizes that they are primarily categories used by the analyst to arrange his observations rather than sharp distinctions which the people of Konduru make in their own minds. Villagers do differentiate between gods and men but these distinctions, blurred by the Hindu doctrines of maya and transmigration, are of degree rather than of kind.

In Konduru there is also no sharp distinction between religion and entertainment. Religious activities provide much of the village entertainment in the forms of festivals, fairs, temple services, and family rites. On the other hand religious myths provide most of the themes for village dramas, dances, and *bajanas*, and their enactment can become a religious experience. Entertainment reaffirms village beliefs and vividly interprets them for children and adults alike, which reinforces the importance of religion in the lives of the people.

While there are many rituals in Konduru in the natural sphere of life and in the area of entertainment, the discussion here will deal largely with those rites which would be considered religious according to Western tradition.

RELIGION

Numerous attempts have been made to distinguish between religion and magic, but no single definition has been agreed upon unanimously. In Konduru, the distinction first made by Sir James Frazer is useful in defining polar types of behavior related to the supernatural. According to Frazer, the essential difference between religion and magic lies in the attitude of the individual. In religion the devotee treats supernatural beings as free agents which he must contact and influence by supplication and worship. The magician, on the other hand, believes that he can control the supernatural beings and forces through specific acts, the correct performance of which, in and of itself, insures the desired results. Rituals, for the most part, have elements that are both religious and magical. The same rite may be religious to one performer and magical to another. Even to the same person, a given rite may be religious on one occasion and magical on another.

High Religion

It is useful in Konduru to distinguish between high religions and low religions. Konduru's high religions include Hinduism, Islam, and Christianity, each of which has its own sacred scriptures, literary creeds, high deities, well-developed institutions, priestly offices, and formal temples. High religions have their own great traditions — those rites and beliefs shared widely by their followers, codified in their scriptures, debated in their literature, and institutionalized in their great shrines and leaders. They also have little traditions — the localized myths and practices encrusting those elements of the great tradition which have filtered down to the level of the village (see Table 15).

Table 15. Patterns of Hindu Supernaturalism in Konduru

High Religion	High Magic
Great Tradition: benevolent Hindu high gods; Sanskritic scriptures; Vedas Upanishads, Epics, etc.; Brahman priests; vegetarian and fire offerings; national shrines and major village temples; cyclic worship rites: Hindu festivals, temple services, and orthodox rites of passage	astrology; some mantras used in formal rites
Little Tradition: regional Hindu gods and local gods linked to Hinduism; vernacular scriptures: caste Puranas, local epics, etc.; Brahman, Tambali, Nambi, and caste priests among varna castes; Dasari and Baine priests among Harijans; vegetarian offerings, some blood sacrifices; local village and household shrines and images; cyclic rites: regional festivals and local *jatras*, building rites, and local variations on life-cycle rites	white magic for curing diseases and guarding children; black magic; shakti worship
Low Religion	Low Magic
local capricious goddesses, demons, powers, etc.; no written scriptures, little institutionalized church; Washerman, Potter, Herdsman, and Leatherworker priests; blood sacrifices frequently required; field and family shrines, little or no use of images sculptured in the human form; crisis rites: during illness, plague, fires, disasters, crop rites: at planting, harvesting, etc.	fortune telling; divination; evil eye

The manifestations of high religion in Konduru are both numerous and obvious. The mosque with its priest draws Muslims to daily prayers and seasonal holidays, and the prayer wall on the edge of the village attracts the faithful of the plateau to the great festivals of Muharram and Ramzan. The tombs of Mahbub Wali, Latif Sahib, Sadānandam, and Mohammed Niranjan Shah Vali are also important in the celebration of Muslim rituals. The Christians, for their part, have a church in one of the hamlets where worship and festivals are arranged by their pastor. It has denominational ties to the Mennonite Brethren churches throughout the state and around the world.

Since most residents of Konduru are Hindus, Hindu rituals in the varna and Harijan communities will be discussed here. The Hindu pantheon has many gods — three hundred and thirty million according to a village proverb. A few, such as Brahma, Vishnu, and Shiva in their many manifestations, are worshiped throughout India. Many, however, are regional or local gods who are only loosely linked to the deities of the Hindu great tradition by local myths. The leading deities are male and have wives, offspring, and supernatural followers. Most are vegetarians, accepting offerings of coconuts, incense, oil, and colored powder from high-caste vegetarian priests who hold offices in temples. These gods participate in the cosmic struggle between good and evil in which the fates of men are determined. They reward the faithful and punish the evildoers; furthermore, their might knows no geographic boundaries.

Konduru has two temples and several shrines open to the Hindus of the varna castes. Until a few decades ago the large Rama temple lay empty and neglected, but today it is the center of most of the village worship as a result of the efforts of Krishna Chari, its hereditary Brahman priest. Newlyweds pause to offer prayers to the gods, devotees gather for weekly *bajanas*, and troubled or thankful worshipers pause to bring their gifts. Each year the temple hosts a religious fair or *jatra* to celebrate the marriage of Rama to Sita. Nearby, Shiva is enshrined in the form of a linga or phallic symbol. Villagers say that he was caught seducing the wife of another god who placed a curse upon him that, henceforth, he would be worshiped only in this form. Many of his followers wear miniature lingas around their necks or enshrine them in their homes, but the Shiva temple is all but deserted. There were two feeble attempts to revive regular worship in the temple in 1964: one was led by a passing mendicant priest who camped in its pillared halls dispensing sacred medicines and another was led by a local Merchant aspiring to village power. Both attempts ended in failure. Other shrines and temples in Konduru and in the nearby forests attract clean-caste worshipers. Despite national laws opening places of worship to people of all castes, these holy places have been closed to Harijans, who have lacked the courage to enter their sacred grounds or join in their annual festivities.

The two large Harijan castes have their own gods and shrines. The Weavers constructed a small temple in honor of Mallikarjuna, who is believed to be an incarnation of Shiva. They also control the large temple of Chenikeshvarudu on the hill beyond the village, which is a shrine of particular importance to them as a symbol of caste power. Three decades ago the high castes possessed the shrine. When the Weavers, who had grown in numbers and power, laid claim to the temple and began attending its annual festival, riots broke out. In court the Weavers claimed that Chenikeshvarudu was their caste deity — a claim that the Muslim judge upheld after a long and bitter litigation. Now only an occasional high-caste man stops to observe the proceedings or sends a gift to the god by the hand of a servant. Jamavanthudu, god of the Leatherworkers, is ensconced in a small rock shrine in the Harijan section of the village. Harijan deities, too, are linked by mythologies to the gods of the Hindu great tradition, and many of the Harijan ceremonies, performed by Harijan priests rather than Brahmans, imitate the Brahmanic rites.

Hindu deities are found in most village homes. Many, such as Srinivas, Subramanya, Satyanarayana, and Venkateshvarudu, are found in homes of all castes. Others are worshiped chiefly by a single caste. Lakshmi, goddess of wealth, is the patron of the Merchants; Lingamayya, god of the forest, belongs to the tribal Chenchu; and Peddamma, goddess of the tigers, is served by the Herdsmen whose cattle are frequent victims of her ire as they graze in the forests. Washermen worship Madel, Gypsies serve Balaji, and many Muslims fear Narsappa, a fierce spirit that possesses people and causes them to go mad. A survey of the homes of five Konduru castes showed that on the average three Hindu and local deities were enshrined in each home (see Table 16).

Low Religion

In Konduru there are a host of supernatural beings that are not linked to any of its literate high religions but are served by members from all of its religious communities. Chief among these are the local and regional goddesses who reside in trees, rocks, streams, and whirlwinds and are enshrined in crude rock shelters in the fields, beside the roads, and in the homes. Capricious and bloodthirsty, they demand the sacrifice of animals to satisfy their desires; therefore, the Brahmans refuse to serve them. Their priests are Washermen, Potters, and Leatherworkers.

Unlike their counterparts in the high religions, the deities of Konduru's low religion have power over only limited territories, generally a radius of five or ten miles from their place of habitation. The same deities, however, are found repeatedly throughout the countryside. All villagers fear their anger which can bring disease and death to those who neglect them, blight to crops, fires to houses, barrenness to wives, and plague

Table 16. Distribution of Deities Enshrined in Konduru Households
according to Caste

Deities	Farmers	Barbers	Washer-men	Weavers	Leather-workers
Hindu deities					
Shiva	3	0	27	0	0
Satyanarayana	10	0	27	0	0
Venkateshvarudu	2	11	27	2	5
Local deities and ancestors					
Veranagamma	5	0	0	0	0
Pinamma	7	0	27	7	6
Yellamma	9	14	19	28	32
Balamma	0	1	12	25	28
Maicamma	0	3	5	3	19
Madel	0	0	27	0	0
Poshamma	0	0	0	2	12
Laxamma	0	0	0	5	0
Bakandu	0	0	0	2	0
Lalamma	0	0	0	1	0
Niranjan	0	0	0	1	0
Ancestors	0	0	0	6	0
Number of homes in each caste...............	10	14	27	31	33
Average number of deities per home..........	3.6	2.1	6.3	2.6	3.1

and drought to the village. Even the local Brahmans who deny their existence take no chances and send their offerings by the hand of a family servant to be sacrificed to the goddesses of their fields.

Maicamma illustrates the nature of Konduru's goddesses. In the form of Fort Maicamma she was enshrined with proper sacrifices when the village citadels of Konduru, Podur, Maradpur, and Rameshvaram were constructed as protection for these villages against external attack. Occasionally she appears in the early dawn in a field as a pale white hand reaching out of the ground, or as a toadstool. If plucked, her sap may run blood red indicating the presence of Bloody Maicamma, bearer of accidents. Sometimes the sap flows white indicating Milky Maicamma,

bearer of diseases, and sometimes it flows clear, a sign of Uppala Maicamma, fiercest of all her apparitions. Most farmers beseech her to move
on by offering her food and sacrifices and by placing a basket over her.
In the few cases in which she refuses to move on, the hapless farmer is
forced to erect a small shelter for her in the field and bring her annual
sacrifices of blood.

Maicamma, like the other goddesses, assists those who are faithful to
her in their worship. Balayya, a prosperous farmer and one of the village magicians, experienced her help after he moved one of the many
Maicammas in the fields around Konduru onto his own land. His care
of her was rewarded after a jewel robbery which took place in 1963.

ᘯᘯThe women of Balayya's household forgot to pick up their jewelry
when they returned from taking their baths in their well outside the
village. When one of the villagers stopped for a drink, he spied the gold
in a niche in the wall and pocketed it. In a moment he was struck blind.
He remembered that Maicamma guarded Balayya's field and well, and,
certain that she was the cause of his misfortune, he promised to return
the jewelry and offer her a chicken. Feeling his way out of the well, he
put the jewelry in the fork of a nearby tree, and his sight returned.
Thoroughly shaken by the experience, the man ran to tell Balayya of
the valuables and gave him money to buy the sacrifice.ᘯᘯ

On another occasion Balayya's brother-in-law stole his new harrow
and became deathly sick. When no medicines would cure him, he
turned to divination and found that the curse of Maicamma was upon
him. He wrote to Balayya and promised to return the implement; shortly
thereafter, he recovered.

Maicamma is demanding. Whenever Balayya buys his wife a new
sari, Maicamma is jealous unless placated with a new dress. And her
displeasure can be costly as Balayya learned in an incident that occurred in 1965.

ᘯᘯ"One day on the way to the fields one of our oxen bloated. The medicines of the local veterinarian did her no good. When we hitched another ox to the cart, he bolted and ran the cart into the hedgerow. We
realized that Maicamma was angry for we had neglected our usual
sacrifice. We called our Washerman and he killed the sacrifice. We
cooked a meal for the goddess and offered her sweets and incense.
Finally we placed small lamps before her. For his services the Washer-

man took the head and forefeet of the goat and we gave him some beer as well." ᘓᘓ

Other goddesses also influence the lives of the villagers. Maicamma has six sisters: Poshamma who causes stomachaches and smallpox; Peddamma the tiger goddess who slays cattle straying in the forest; Yellamma who brings sores and blindness; Balamma who causes mothers to lack milk and infants to die; Mankarlamma, the goddess of the Brassworkers, and Edamma. These seven are guarded by their brother, Pota Raju. Earth Lakshmamma inhabits the soil; Cowshed Lakshmamma lives in the cattle sheds; Gangamma resides in rivers and wells; Pinna Devata occupies Washermen homes; and Nagamma, goddess of the cobras, lives in anthills. Bhavanamma causes headaches, Sandla Saudamma guards hidden treasures, and Grama Devata the Village Goddess protects the village. In addition there are ghosts, demons, devils, female ghouls, spirits, winds, and powers without number (for a partial listing of the supernatural beings of Konduru see Appendix II).

The line between the deities of Konduru's high religion and those of the low is not always sharp, and Balayya, like other villagers, switches easily in his worship from one to the other. He worships the Hindu gods with the aid of his Brahman priest and turns to worship the goddesses assisted by his family Washerman or Potter. The goodwill of all is necessary for his health and safety, the prosperity of his endeavors, and the well-being of his household.

The caste system extends upward to include the hierarchy of gods and downward to embrace the world of animals and plants (see Figure 17). The beliefs that the world is illusory or maya and that all life is caught in an almost unending cycle of death and rebirth blur even those boundaries dividing gods from men and men from animals. The step between saints and demigods is a half step and pictures of great men such as Mahatma Gandhi and John F. Kennedy appear in a household shrine beside those of Vishnu or Shiva. This concept of the universe which arranges all life along a single continuum sharply contrasts with the world of Western man which has sharp boundaries dividing life into discrete categories that differ in kind as well as degree.

MAGIC

Magic pervades both the high and the low religious systems of Konduru. It appears sometimes in the form of a mantra or sacred chant

which combines prayers with certain powerful sounds such as *hrēm,*
kshaum, klēm, ram, and *phat.* The proper intonation of a mantra in and
of itself controls the supernatural powers. Some sounds such as *ōm* and
svaha are particularly powerful. *Ōm* is learned by the beginning pupil
on the first day of instruction in the traditional class taught by the village guru and traced in the sand in the shade of a large tree. If learned

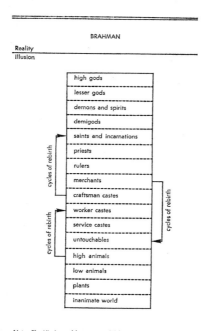

BRAHMAN

Reality
Illusion

| high gods |
| lesser gods |
| demons and spirits |
| demigods |
| saints and incarnations |
| priests |
| rulers |
| merchants |
| craftsman castes |
| worker castes |
| service castes |
| untouchables |
| high animals |
| low animals |
| plants |
| inanimate world |

cycles of rebirth

cycles of rebirth

cycles of rebirth

Note: The Hindu world view sees all life as essentially of one kind.
Differences between the phenomenal varieties of life are
differences of degree rather than of kind. Those above have
more spirit and less matter and those below have more matter and less spirit.

17. The Hindu world view of life

properly, it is thought to guarantee true wisdom to the student. Com-
bining the first and last letters of the alphabet, *ōm* includes all sounds,
language, writings, and sacred scriptures. It was the first sound heard
in the universe and is the proper introduction to most mantras. *Svaha,*
according to the villagers, means may they be burned to ashes, and is
a closing imprecation in many mantras.

Mantras are important in Hindu rituals. Sometimes they appear as
prayers and other times they can be considered magical chants. Their
unending cadence recited by the officiating priest is punctuated here

and there by proper gestures, by offerings of sacred leaves, incense, fire, water, and spices, and by band music. Mantras also permeate the low magical rites that pervade village life. In its low form magic is commonly used to cure diseases and to guard against dangers such as the poisonous viper.

&& Balayya, one of Konduru's most powerful magicians, was explaining the intricacies of the jajmani system one evening when a small but deadly viper crawled out from beneath the observer's cot upon which the two were seated. After calling his servant and ordering him to kill the serpent, Balayya bent down and, taking care not to miss any toward the tip of the tail, counted the stripes across the viper's back. Only then did he offer an explanation. As a powerful magician he could not take life without losing his power. Moreover, to cure a man bitten by that snake he would have to know the exact number of stripes across its back. For each stripe he would recite the following mantra seven times and smear his forehead with white ash as he did so.

> *Ōm Garabaranābhava–Sarva peshāchādi gruhamulu*
> Ōm, O Birthless Garavara, All evil spirits and planets
> *nanu dzūchi–bhayamondi–paradzudu.*
> having seen me, being afraid, may they look askance.
> *Em, ksham, shaum, svaha.*
> (powerful sounds). &&

Some magicians achieve widespread fame for their cures of snakebite. Konduru villagers occasionally turn to a Muslim magician in the city of Hyderabad whose powerful Urdu mantras are effective throughout the state. A letter or telegram informing the magician of a crisis is enough. By his powers he divines the type of snake involved and recites appropriate chants. If he senses that these mantras are ineffectual, he incants a particularly powerful one — one which will cause the snake to return, bite the victim again, and suck out its own poison. As a result, the snake dies and the patient is cured. People believe that every time he uses this mantra a few days are taken from his life on earth.

A second form of magic uses yantras or powerful symbols (see Figure 18). These may be written on paper and tied to the body, inscribed in copper and encased in silver amulets, or penned on paper and boiled in water which is then drunk. Yantras utilize powerful sounds in their written form. Like mantras they are used to heal sickness, cure snakebites, exorcise spirits, heal scorpion stings, guard against the evil eye,

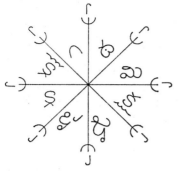

YANTRA USED FOR MALARIA

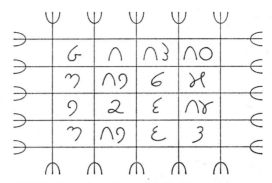

YANTRA FOR ASSURING CONCEPTION INVOLVES IN-
SCRIBING IT ON A PIECE OF PAPER OR COPPER SHEET-
ING AND TYING IT TO THE ARM OF THE BARREN
WOMAN.

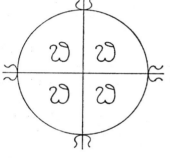

YANTRA FOR A HEADACHE INCLUDES WRITING IT ON A
BRASS PLATE, LIGHTING A CANDLE BEFORE IT AFTER IT
IS WRAPPED IN STRING, COVERING IT WITH RED AND
YELLOW POWDERS, AND TYING IT TO THE HEAD.

YANTRA TO THE GOD NARASIMHA
FOR POWER AND GENERAL
PROTECTION

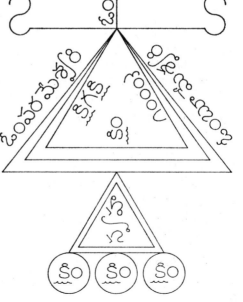

18. Yantras used on the
Konduru plateau

141

induce easy birth, produce virility in men and pregnancy in women, cure headaches, and drive off body pains. Some induce passionate love and others bring plagues upon wayward husbands, while still others guard the wearer against all dangers in general.

In addition to mantras and yantras there are other forms of magic. There are various medicines (*mandu*) made from ground tigers' teeth, crushed human skulls, and saps from various trees. There are specific actions such as blowing, fanning, and tapping.

The simple household magic used by older women to cure minor diseases and ease childbirth requires little knowledge, but the powerful magic practiced by Balayya and several other men of Konduru involves many restrictions. Following secret instruction at the hand of a guru, the candidate undergoes an initiation rite. Balayya had to stand in a well, reciting mantras while dipping himself in the cold water during an eclipse of the moon. Others reportedly live for years in the forest without washing their bodies. Some apprentices, villagers claim, live among the tombs and must touch their tongues to the menstrual blood of a Leatherworker virgin to validate their power.

To keep his power a magician must observe numerous taboos. He must never treat a pregnant woman, for the unborn fetus will draw away his power. He must avoid certain foods and spices. If, while eating, he sees a snake, a rope, a Washerman, a corpse, a scorpion, or any other of a long list of forbidden objects, or even hears them mentioned in speech, he must leave the meal unfinished and fast until the next meal.

Magicians, for the most part, practice white or beneficial magic, but those who know its secrets are often charged with performing evil magic (*chethavardu*). Balayya was charged with killing a child in 1966, and a Konduru Herdsman known for his powerful magic has reportedly killed three men in the past few years. The magician frequently uses a piece of hair, clothing, or feces from the victim to place a curse upon him. He may form an image of the victim, or resort to the use of various forms of medicines. Village wives are frequently charged with utilizing black magic against wayward husbands. In 1964, such a case occurred with a jealous wife and was related to me by Balayya shortly thereafter.

&&"Somayya had moved recently from Deverakonda to Konduru. When he returned to Deverakonda for long periods of time, his wife became suspicious and accused him of unfaithfulness. He, of course, denied the charge; so when he continued to visit Deverakonda, she resorted to magic. She mixed some medicines made from tree barks and various powders and put them secretly into his food. In his stomach the medicines formed a hard ball that sent out roots. His food would not digest and he became weak like a woman who had just delivered a child.

"To find out the cause for his weakness Somayya went to a diviner. The man poured out sap into Somayya's palm and when it turned black and solid they knew that he was under a curse. In the palm of a bystander the same sap remained like water. The diviner gave Somayya medicines to swallow and began to recite the names of those who might have placed the curse upon him. When the diviner spoke the name of the wife, Somayya threw up the ball. Fortunately, it came out young and green and the man was cured. Sometimes, if it has grown too long, part of it stays in the stomach and the man dies. Somayya sent his wife off to her home. Perhaps when he is not so angry he will take her back again." ᛉᛉ

The only cure for a curse is a more powerful mantra; neither local herbal medicines, of which there are many, nor Western medicines are of any use. To punish a magician who continues to cause evil one only needs to knock out his front teeth so that he can no longer pronounce his mantras correctly or smear feces and urine upon his lips.

A mild form of evil power that plagues certain people from birth is *dishti* or the evil eye. People with an evil eye make cooked food being eaten by another indigestible just by looking at it. Their gaze also brings accidents upon children unprotected by suitable yantras. Brides and grooms, who are particularly susceptible to the evil eye, must be protected during the marriage ceremonies with special headdresses.

Divination (*anjanam*) is frequently used to determine the causes of strange events, unusual accidents and deaths, or to foretell the future. A specialized form of divination, known as *dhanapesāchi*, is used to locate and extract gold believed to be buried in ancient temples, forts, cemeteries, and other unusual places. Such treasures are guarded by spirits or the ghosts of their dead owners and proper rites are necessary to protect the taker from plagues and death. Ancient palm-leaf manuscripts still found in the villages give directions for locating this gold as well as the mantras needed to extract it. Excerpts from one such document found in Konduru read as follows:

Prerequisites for the Exploration of Treasures

Saints of god, ascetics, mendicants, hermits, poets of divine inspiration, and such people are qualified to dig up a treasure hidden underground. Only people void of base impulses such as hatred and pride, those who do not swerve from the path of truth, and those who practice penance should venture out for treasures. Swarthy and tall people, abnormally sized ones, physically, are divinely ordained for such purposes. They should be bold and courageous, interested in divine oracles, devotees of Shiva, self-controlled. Those who are untrustworthy, filled with guile, unfaithful in religious rituals, covetous and stealthy, gossips and scandalmongers, should not be taken into such ventures. Moreover, people who sleep during the day and keep awake at night, like owls, should not accompany the devotee on his expedition. If paupers, sickly ones, and sinners so much as see the ceremony, the treasure will never appear.

Now there are specific places where one can expect a treasure: (1) old reservoirs, (2) old and antiquated gardens, (3) burial and cremation grounds, (4) places of religious pilgrimage and interest, (5) places haunted by celestial beings and demigods, (6) within rock pillars of old buildings, and (7) caves wherein hermits have lived. These are the places where you are sure to excavate treasures.

Particularly one should look in temple ruins where idols lie broken and devastated. In such places, look for these signs to be sure a treasure is present. If the head of the idol is chopped off, look near the hands. Ten marks there will show you that a treasure lies within. If the thigh is broken, search beneath the hand for one of the following signs. Six marks, black spots, somewhere on the body of the image are a sign that you can find six hundred gold coins within. . . .

If the idol is eight-handed, it has a treasure beneath. Certain herbs must be used: the bitter cucumber, the prickly poppy, and the thorn apple must be ground together and smeared onto the earth. The mantra to be chanted on this occasion is the one invoking the god Ranga. "Ōm, Oh Ranga, presiding deity over treasure, dispeller of obstacles, Svaha."

If the statue is that of Chinmayya, god of internal bliss, and if the statue shows him to be clothed with silk, you must break open the stomach to find the treasure. Apply to the stomach of the figure the following herbs ground into an ointment: long peppers, black peppers, and cow's urine. A mantra should be chanted to give strength to the ointment so that the stomach will be broken. "Ōm, praise to you, oh god. You who appear as Vasudeva, as the universal Anjana. Oh one without

form who takes form at pleasure, protector of the world. Ōm, Svaha."
This mantra will break the unbreakable.

Belief in astrology is also widespread. The intersection of the moment
of birth and the cycles of the moon, planets, and sun determine for each
man both the auspicious and dangerous times for specific ventures. Horoscopes are read by the village Brahman and others are versed in the art
with the aid of books known as *panchangams*. Most villagers are content
to seek propitious occasions for the major events in life such as marriage,
but one informant consulted his *panchangam* each time he visited me.

Omens are also used to discern good and evil fortunes, particularly
for those going on long journeys, for those making preliminary arrangements for a bride, and for those entering new ventures. The nature of
these omens is well illustrated by a local maxim:

A Washerman's bundle, a cat fight, a cloud of smoke, a coal basket, a
carded cotton basket, a crazy man, a Mondi, a noseless person, a bundle
of sticks, a bundle of skins, a Tambali, a Sanyasin, an ancient person, a
single cart wheel, a loose well wheel, a fox's howl, a tortoise, a whirl-
wind, someone returning from the water with an empty pot, an owl's
cry, a naked adult, a childless woman, a leper, a person sick unto death,
a rabbit; these, if any you see, do not make a journey, not even to the
gods.

It is obvious that none can be so strict, but many important journeys are
made at night to avoid the sight of such omens.

According to villagers, professional magicians from the Mondi caste
tour the villages challenging local magicians to duels of strength. A coconut, a bowl, an egg, and an idol with a coin in its mouth are placed in
a row. The Mondi must carry each back across the base line while the
local magicians use their powers to stop him. They beat logs causing
him to fall writhing to the ground. They pluck strings on bows and his
skin splits and blood flows. They conjure up snakes or turn the objects
into water which cannot be carried. At each turn the Mondi, aided by
his fellows, counters with other magic.

Even more than magic the villagers fear the power of Shaktis, the
most powerful of supernatural forces. Shaktis, if they appear at all, are
seen as fearsome, bloodthirsty creatures with three fiery eyes and fangs
holding battle-axes in one hand and swords in the other. In the past
they demanded human sacrifice. Konduru's Bangle Pulayya was struck
blind by a Shakti, and although he knew the relative who sent the evil,

he dared not seek revenge, for mantras have no effect against those who control Shaktis.

Religious rituals dramatize the way Konduru villagers view their world. Not only do rituals portray the relationships which link men to the other inhabitants of the universe, both natural and supernatural, but they also reaffirm the social order of men. They reinforce the values of groups and communities and provide them with a sense of solidarity and power. Moreover, changes within the social order are finally validated when they lead to corresponding changes in the rituals of the village. To the individual, rituals provide a sense of order and access to supernatural powers, which are needed to combat the disrupting uncertainties of life and, thus, give him a feeling of reassurance and security.

Rituals mark the boundaries between the religious communities of Konduru. They also dramatize the differences between castes. Nowhere are the subcultural distinctions between castes so vividly portrayed as in the unending varieties of rites and ceremonies performed in the village.

Confirmatory Rites

The distinction which Evans Pritchard makes (1956) between confirmatory rites and piacular rites is useful in analyzing rituals in Konduru. Confirmatory rites, he says, are concerned with changes in the social status of individuals and the interaction of social groups. The term is roughly equivalent to rites of passage, as originally used by Van Gennep and later translated by Beattie as transition rituals. Van Gennep argued that simple societies ritualize any change from one state to another — changes in the status of the individual, or changes in seasons, residence sites, etc. In recent times, however, the term rites of passage has come to refer to those rites such as birth, puberty, marriage, and death which mark the transition of an individual from one status to another. It is in this sense that the term is used here.

RITES OF PASSAGE

Few ceremonies illustrate the elaboration of rituals so well as marriage. Each step is taken with the enactment of the proper rituals, from the first plans for acquiring a bride, to the determination of an auspicious time for the ceremony by the family priest, to the procession that will escort the bride to her new home. A brief description of a Merchant marriage ceremony illustrates the complexity of the rituals.

Arrangements for the ceremony begin on a propitious day with the construction of a pandal in front of the bride's house which is decorated with flowers, banana plants, and mango leaves. After pieces of turmeric, nine kinds of grain, and some coins are tied to the wedding pole, the household gods and ancestors are invoked to attend the ceremony. Women of the household perform certain rites known as *strī achar* or women's rites (for the Telugu names for the ceremonies and a list of marriage rites from various castes see Appendix III). Five married women whose husbands are living pound rice on a mortar with two wooden pestles bound together and adorned with pieces of turmeric and betel leaves. They grind turmeric and rice flour for use in the wedding. A procession fetches ceremonial pots from the Potters' hamlet which are then decorated. Two large pots are filled with water and lamps are floated inside. Rites associated with the land (*deshachār*) follow next. These include gifts and offerings to local goddesses and cobras. Other preliminary rites include the welcoming ceremony described earlier and a rite in which oil and turmeric are given to the guests. The bride and groom are then smeared with turmeric.

The wedding begins when the bridal couple are brought to the pandal wearing their wedding finery and elaborate headdresses to guard them against the evil eye. Cooked rice and curds are waved before the face of the groom and thrown to the evil spirits to arrest their baneful influence.

The orthodox Hindu rites (*shastriyāchār*) begin with the investment of the groom with the sacred thread of the twice-born which entitles him to take a wife and become a householder. Then the marriage ceremonies begin. While a silk cloth is draped between the bride and groom to the chant of mantras, the audience joins the priest in throwing rice upon them. After the bride and groom throw cumin seed and jaggery upon each other and tread lightly upon each other's feet the curtain is raised and they are seated opposite each other. The groom places the bride's hand in the hollow of his own. Then the bride's mother pours cold water into the palm of her husband's hand which he in turn pours into his daughter's hand from where it trickles through the groom's hand to the plate below — this ceremony symbolizes the gift of the girl by her father to the groom. The groom ties thread bracelets and a marriage necklace on the bride to seal the marriage. The bride is seated beside her new husband and their clothes are knotted together. The major ceremonies are concluded as the audience throws more rice upon the couple.

After the wedding, guests bring gifts which are carefully recorded by a secretary, for now the couple has entered the caste network of gift exchange. At some future dates the couple will be expected to repay with comparable gifts at the weddings of the children of the donors. They also join in the feast and processions through the village which publicly announce the marriage and display the wealth and power of the family and caste. The priest shows the new couple the North Star, an emblem of marital constancy, and they visit the village temple.

Many ceremonies of a more local nature, known as caste rites (*kulāchār*), follow. After the couple is smeared with oil by the Barber, his wife pours water over them. The groom offers alms to the three hundred thirty million gods, while intentionally making mistakes in his calculations which his brother-in-law corrects. He also worships two small boats floating in a pot, which is supposed to symbolize river trade. The bridal pair are seated on a platform amid a beautiful pattern traced in five colors on the floor, as the bride's parents march five times around them to symbolize the visits between the families. Of the many other rites, one is of particular interest. Following offerings of betel, powders, necklaces, food, and flowers to the goddess Gauramma, the couple enacts a drama of domestic life which creates a great deal of amusement for all. The new wife gives a small sandalwood doll representing her child to the husband and asks him to care for it while she attends to other domestic affairs. He soon returns it and claims that he must attend to business. The rounds of ceremonies, each performed with appropriate mantras, offerings, sprinklings, gestures, and music, continue until the final feast generally held on the sixteenth day after the wedding.

A comparison of marriage ceremonies between castes points out the mixed origins of the rituals as well as the cultural distinctions between castes (see Table 17). While the higher castes tend to follow more closely the orthodox ceremonies prescribed by Manu, certain of these such as Antapāt, Kankana Bandha, and Kanyādan are practiced even by the Harijans (see Appendix III). Some orthodox rites like Edurukolu are enacted by the high castes, while others like Vivāha Homam, Shesha Homam, and Saptapadi are performed only by the Konduru Brahmans.

Some ceremonies such as Nagavelli and Pampu are regional in na-

Table 17. Common Rites of the Marriage Ceremony Practiced by Certain Konduru Castes

Rites Found in the Hindu Great Tradition	Brahmans	Merchants	Farmers	Winetappers	Washermen	Harijan Weavers
Punyachana Nandi Sradha Grahamakha	Punyachana Nandi Sradha Grahamakha	Kottanam Araveni Kundalu	Kottanam Araveni Kundalu	Kottanam Araveni Kundalu	Kottanam Araveni Kundalu	Kottanam Araveni Kundalu
Mandapa Devati Pratishthapan Vakdan Vagnishachaya	Mandapa Devati Pratishthapan Vakdan Vagnishachaya	Vara Nischaya	Vara Nischaya Prathanam Chyupvidam	?	Deshachar Prathanam	Deshachar Vara Nischaya Prathanam
Simanta Puja Varaprasthan	Simanta Puja Varaprasthan	Edurukolu	Edurukolu			
Madhupark	Madhupark Lagnam	Madhupark Lagnam Padghattanam Jiragudam Kanyadan	Lagnam Padghattanam Jiragudam Kanyadan Mutya Pola	Madhupark Lagnam Padghattanam Jiragudam Kanyadan Mutya Pola	Lagnam Padghattanam Jiragudam Kanyadan	Lagnam Padghattanam Jiragudam Kanyadan
Antapat Kanyadan	Antapat Kanyadan					
Kankana Bandha Vivaha and Laji Homam	Kankana Bandha Vivaha and Laji Homam	Kankana Bandha	Pusti Mittalu Tilabalabium	Pusti Mittalu Tilabalabium	Pusti Mittalu Tilabalabium	Pusti Mittalu Tilabalabium
Saptapadi Shesha Homam	Saptapadi Shesha Homam Ankur Rupanam Sadasu Nagavelli Dandya	Talval Brahmamodi Arundhati Dharshanam Mailapolu Vadibiyam Nagavelli Navagradha Puja Kanka Visarjan Sade	Talval Brahmamodi Arundhati Dharshanam Mailapolu Vadibiyam Nagavelli	Talval Brahmamodi Arundhati Dharshanam Mailapolu Vadibiyam Nagavelli	Talval Brahmamodi Arundhati Dharshanam Vadibiyam Nagavelli	Talval Brahmamodi Arundhati Dharshanam Vadibiyam Nagavelli
Sumukha Sade	Sumukha Sade					
Laxmi Puja Devakothapan Mandapothapan	Laxmi Puja Devakothapan Mandapothapan	Appagintha Padhari Panduga	Appagintha	Appagintha	Appagintha	Appagintha

149

ture. They are observed by most castes in the Telugu-speaking areas of southern India. Other regional rites such as Mailapolu are practiced only by a few castes. Interestingly enough, there appears to be a greater difference between the ritual patterns of the Brahmans and the Merchants than there is between those of the Merchants and the Shudras. There are also major differences in the observation of rites between the varna castes and the Harijans.

Finally, certain rites are unique to specific castes. The Merchants observe Kanka Visarja and the Farmers perform Nischitartha. Even in the same rite there are specific variations from caste to caste. The Merchants worship ships of trade and the Farmers propitiate plows. In the Kanyādan ceremony the high castes have the bride's father offer the groom a mixture of honey and clarified butter; however, in the low castes the bride's father and mother wash the groom's feet.

A similar analysis could be made of other rites of passage. Birth ceremonies differ markedly from the elaborate Brahmanic rites observed by the priestly castes to the simpler rites practiced by the low castes. Marginal castes and tribesmen differ even more in their observances. The transient Soothsayers, for example, practice a form of couvade in which the husband goes to bed after his wife delivers the child, and she returns to work. Some castes observe puberty rites for the girls. Others mark the transition of boys to adulthood. Even for death the rites differ greatly. Some bury face down, some bury face up, some bury seated, some bury in salt, and some, chiefly the high castes, practice cremation. It is in the detailed analysis of rites that the cultural differences between castes become most obvious.

Rites of passage not only mark the transition of an individual from one status to another, but also reinforce the social networks of the village. Jajmani ties are strengthened, for the family's Goldsmith, Ironsmith, Carpenter, Washerman, Barber, Leatherworker, and Weaver all have indispensable parts in the ceremonies. Caste and village ties are renewed as guests join in the feasting and festivities.

CYCLIC RITES

Certain ceremonies in Konduru are cyclic, that is, they occur in the normal course of events at regular intervals. In high-caste homes as well as in a few devout low-caste ones day-to-day worship is conducted before the household deities enshrined along the southern or western walls of the house. There are also annual festivities in honor of important ancestors. During Petramasa the low castes observe a month of honor for the dead, including one day for special ceremonies and a feast. The twice-born remember deceased relatives on Tadinum, the anniversary dates of their departure.

Some cyclic rites involve larger numbers of people from a single caste or religious community. Informal *bajanas* are held weekly in the Rama temple and *rathams* or worship services are arranged in the name of a Hindu god by a thankful devotee dedicating a new house, or celebrating a miraculous cure.

The most prominent cyclic rites are the festivals marking the changes in seasons and years, or celebrating the rites of passage in the lives of the gods. Konduru Hindus observe such all-India festivals as Dasara, Divali, Holi, Shiva Ratri, and Vinayaka Chauti; some of which are associated with local practices and interpretations. Divali is traditionally associated with Rama's triumphant return to Ayodhya following his exile, but local villagers use the festival to celebrate the death of the tyrant Narakasu by the hand of Satya Devi. Throughout much of India, Dasara honors Rama's triumph over Ravana. Konduru villagers, however, on that day recall the return of the exiled Pandavas to the Jami tree which hid their magical bows by turning them into leaves. Konduru men of the higher castes escort Rama from the temple to the Jami trees. There, on pieces of paper, they write mantras which express their wishes for the coming year:

> With the Jami leaf may my sins be removed, my enemies destroyed, as if by Arjuna's and Rama's bows.
> Oh Jami, whose beauty is that of the lotus, as we touch your sacred leaves, we will have long life.
> In the year Vishva Vasu; the month Ashvayuja; the cycle of the full moon, the tenth day, we met you.
> Grant me this year a blessing worth one million rupees.

The papers are placed in the hollow of the Jami tree by the Brahman family priest while Krishna Chari, the temple priest, leads the Rama worship nearby. Men exchange Jami leaves as a sign of friendship and those bearing grudges are urged to forget their differences, at least for a season. In the exchange, low-ranked men bow before their superiors as a mark of respect.

Festivals like Ugadi and Sankranti have a regional distribution. On the Ugadi or Telugu New Year's Day, craftsmen worship their tools, Barbers their knives, Washermen their washing stones and firepots, Weavers their looms, and Leatherworkers their tanning vats. Drivers garland their trucks and buses. On this day field work may be begun for the new crops. Farmers go to their fields bearing small baskets of fertilizer, hoes, pots of water and food, and burning coals. There they decorate their implements with mango leaves and vermilion and turmeric spots and then offer fire and water to them. Each farmer cuts a few weeds and so begins the work for a new year. He eats the sweetmeats and returns home in silence. Thrice the ceremony is repeated. Merchants take stock of their wares and give out only needed supplies, which are to be paid for at a later date. Near the temple the Brahman astrologer consults his almanac and as the men gather round he predicts the fortunes of the coming year. Will there be rain? How will the prices fluctuate?

Sankranti, like other festivals, has many related myths. Konduru villagers generally tell the story of Balachakravarthi.

ᘘᘘBalachakravarthi was a great emperor renowned for his honesty and justice. The gods decided to test his goodness and take away some of his power which was becoming greater than their own. When Vishnu appeared as a dwarf begging at his court, the king, not knowing the divine nature of the deformed man and being too noble to turn him away, asked him to make his request. "Give me the land upon which I can place my foot thrice," asked the beggar. "Is that all; then go measure it out," said the emperor as he reached for the Kamandalam jug to pour out water to seal the promise. The court guru, understanding the trick, turned himself into a frog and blocked the spout, but the noble emperor, not suspecting trickery, poked the obstruction aside with an arrow. Immediately the dwarf turned himself into a giant. With his first foot he covered the earth and with the second he covered the heavens. Turning to the king he asked where he could find room for the third step promised to him. "There is no place left but my head," said the emperor, "so place your foot upon it." Thereupon Vishnu stepped upon the emperor and pushed him down into hell where he became ruler of the netherworld. But for his saintliness and honesty the gods granted his request to return each year to visit the earth on Sankranti.ᘘᘘ

Some festivals in Konduru are observed by only the higher castes. On Chiluka Dvādashi local Brahmans and Merchants select cows from their herds for worship. Women make hoof prints with white flour upon the freshly dunged entranceways to their homes. Then families offer jaggery to the decorated cows and distribute the remainder among themselves as a sacred food. On Nagula Panchami the same castes fast and offer foods to cobras living in anthills, on Toli Ekadashi they honor Vishnu, on Narasimha Jayanti they worship Narasimha, and on Kartika Purnami they venerate the Tulsi tree. Other festivals are observed only by the Brahmans. Vasant Panchami and Rath Saptami honor Shiva, and Ananta Chaturdasi is in memory of Vishnu. On Neela Gauri, Brahman women worship the wife of Shiva with sprouts of nine kinds of grain. Harijans and low Shudras have their own festivals in honor of their caste deities and for many of the village goddesses.

Konduru's most important festival is Sri Rama Navami which commemorates the marriage of Rama and Sita. For eight days and nights people of the varna castes from across the plateau gather at the Rama temple in a religious fair (*jatra*) to celebrate. Days are spent in visiting friends who have gathered from other villages. Vendors ply their wares from temporary shelters of burlap or leaves: stalls sell foodstuffs, "hotels" dispense tea and coffee, and shops display jewelry, religious objects, and toys to catch the eyes of the idle crowds. Days are spent in private worship (*pūja*) and a steady stream of devotees goes to the temple. Worshipers pause to put turmeric and vermilion on the Hanuman guarding the doorway, to ring the bell before the Garuda Pillar, to bow to lesser deities enshrined around the pillared hall, and to give their offerings of coconuts, coins, and incense to the priest who offers them to the gods and returns a portion to each worshiper.

Nights are times for public ceremonies and entertainment. On successive nights Rama is prepared for the wedding, respect is paid to Naga, king of the snakes, and the gods are taken in procession through the streets. On the third afternoon, Rama is dressed as a woman and escorted through the streets to carry out his secret investigations concerning Sita, his bride to be. The same night the sacred fire ceremonies are conducted, and the Edurukolu takes place. Rama, having been escorted through the village, is met by Sita upon his return to the temple. Villagers join one party or the other. With much pleading and jesting each party takes its turn to advance a few feet. Someone in Rama's party calls for Sita to come quickly; then it would be a "love marriage," and everyone laughs. Finally in a burst of cheers the parties meet. Sandalwood powder is thrown in the air as a sign of goodwill. An aged Courtesan woman circles the gods three times to guard them from the evil eye and leads them back to the temple.

The marriage takes place on the fourth day. After more processions through the village the gods are brought to the temple. There Krishna Chari performs the wedding, chanting Sanskrit mantras, propitiating the sacred fire, and enacting the detailed rites. Then the people crowding around bring their gifts to the newlywed deities.

Processions of celebration continue on the following nights. Rama and Sita are paraded through the village on one night seated upon the great brass image of Hanuman. The next night marks the climax of the *jatra* as the gods are pulled through the village in the temple car following the fire rituals. The large multitiered vehicle, newly decorated with paint, mango leaves, and colored tissue, is pulled back and forth on its great stone wheels through the village streets bearing the gods and their attendant priests. The pulsating drums, the clanging bells, the psychedelic flaming of the torches, the overbearing pungency of the incense, and the shouting and surging mob turn the night into a happening. Only as dawn breaks in the eastern sky are the gods returned to their inner sanctum for another year, and the revelers drift home to rest. There are two more nights of ceremonies — those for Nagavelli and the theft of Sita's jewels — but these are anticlimactic, and the worshipers begin to jolt home in their oxcarts.

Konduru's *jatra* unites the clean-caste Hindu communities of the plateau in a common cause. The powerful Harijan Weavers of the same region unite for their own *jatra* at Rayalgundi beyond Konduru. Other *jatras* abound in the nearby plains and attract devotees from the plateau. The ancient shrine of Uma Maheshvaram, carved into the hills near Maradpur, hosts a regional *jatra* that attracts tens of thousands of worshipers for many miles around. Rock inscriptions at the site trace this religious fair back to at least A.D. 1268. A new *jatra*, started in 1961 near Nagerkurnool on the plains, has begun to attract followers from the plateau. It is a small replica of the great temple of Tirupathi near Madras which attracted the rich of the plateau in the past. Today, even the poor visit the new shrine to fulfill their vows to Venkateshvarudu and to celebrate their marriages. The dream of many villagers, however, is to attend the great *jatra* of Shiva held on Shiva Ratri at the nationally famous Shri Salem temple in the forests to the south. There they stand in awe and look at the great temples and observe the strange customs of people from distant places.

Muslims have their own family rites, their festivals, and their religious fairs. The latter, known as *durgas*, commemorate the passing of some great Muslim saint. Disciples of Latif Sahib, the saint of Konduru, hold an annual procession to his grave bearing prayer flags and offerings of food, garlands, and incense. The leaders chant prayers from the Koran as the tomb is covered with new silk cloths. Hindu bypassers pause to crack coconuts and say a prayer. Other *durgas* in Konduru are held in honor of Mahabub Wali and Sadanandam, great Muslim saints of Arabia and northern India, whose tombs are found in many of the villages on the plateau. The great *durga* of Mahammed Niranjan Shah Vali, an Afghan saint who lived in the courts of Pratapa Rudra in the thirteenth century, is located near the Uma Maheshvaram temple and attracts many thousands from throughout the region. In this *durga* the Muslim leaders of Konduru have the right to lead the first of three great processions to the tomb. Worship continues for several days as families slaughter their goats in the surrounding fields and prepare feasts to be shared with the departed saint.

Confirmatory rites provide a sense of order in nature and in the universe for the people of the Konduru plateau. They cut across caste and village boundaries to bridge periodically the cleavages that develop in the workaday world. Because religious instruction is merged with entertainment and the ritual enactment with the social and economic order, the ceremonies reinforce the patterns of Konduru culture. In their performance they also dramatize the unity, or disunity, of the village.

Piacular Rites

Piacular rites, according to Evans-Pritchard, who borrowed the term from Durkheim, are rites performed in situations of danger or crisis. Unlike confirmatory rites, which maintain order in the lives of individuals, nature, and the universe and are themselves predictable, these crisis rites deal with events that threaten unexpectedly to disrupt the order.

In Konduru, confirmatory rites are largely the domain of castes and communities, and are linked to the gods of the high religions. In contrast, crisis rites usually involve individuals and families or the village as a whole, and are frequently linked with the spirits and deities of Konduru's low religion.

Plagued by disease, unexpected deaths, repeated accidents, or strange events, the villager often turns to divination to determine the causes. One or two diviners living in Konduru use the upper grindstone from a grain mill to determine the source of evil. Under possession of a clairvoyant spirit the medium rocks the stone to-and-fro in a heap of rice while the victim recites the names of suspected deities, powers, and persons. When the right name has been recited, the stone becomes rigid in the hands of the diviner. By these same means the diviner can discern what the offended spirit demands in propitiation.

Some castes like the Soothsayers are known to be powerful fortune-tellers and diviners. Their women frequent the village carrying date baskets and their patron goddess Yellamma in the form of a plate embossed with cowrie shells. They tell the future for a few coins. In difficult cases people turn to them for guidance. Bathed and under the possession of a spirit, the Soothsayer sits facing a small lamp playing her musical instrument while the names of deceased relatives, spirits, and gods are recited by the victim, one by one, until the flickering flame becomes steady. Other fortune-tellers use drops of black sap on a leaf to see into the past or future.

Having ascertained the cause of their distress, the victims of a crisis resort to sacrifices at the appropriate shrines and make vows to propitiate the spirit involved, or use yantras and magic to guard themselves from its power.

A crisis may strike a whole village. Prolonged drought, epidemics, plagues of fires, and loss of village strength are signs of supernatural displeasure. Then the village Navel Stone (*bord rayi*), a small stone-lined hole in the street near the Hanuman shrine, and the village boundaries become the center of village crisis rites. These rituals almost took place during the fire plague that swept Konduru in 1965.

ᘓᘓNo one was suspicious when the first thatched roof caught fire. The summer was hot and roofs were dry as tinder. But when two more caught fire the next day, and two on the third, people became fearful. When one of the village diviners declared that the goddess Maicamma was angry, the elders began to make arrangements for the rituals necessary to placate her. Two more houses burned the fifth day, but a couple of lads had been seen near the scene with pans commonly used to carry live coals from one kitchen to another. The elders gave the boys severe warnings and turned them over to the custody of their parents. The crisis rites were delayed to await the outcome. When no further fires started, the villagers were satisfied that the affair was closed. No rites were needed.&&

When plagues strike a village, as they did in one of the nearby villages in 1964, every resident is required to contribute toward the purchase of a sacrificial animal. For any household to refuse is to jeopardize the village as a whole. In a village procession (*grāma kattu*) the beast is led to the boundaries of the village where it is slain, cooked with rice, and offered to the offended goddess. Certain fruits and ox bones are buried on the western edge of the village, and the deity is entreated to move on. Villagers assert that if these measures failed, as they sometimes did in the past, the elders would institute a watch beside the Navel Stone. Outsiders were forbidden to enter the village and worship continued until the danger passed.

Occasionally goddesses pass through the land. They reside in the west or south; hence, none should sleep with his feet pointed in these directions. When such deities go on a journey, they generally arrive from the west. Word precedes their arrival as they pass through villages to the west. When they arrive, village elders choose three auspicious days a week apart from each other on which villagers will take their foodstuffs and cook them on the eastern boundary of the village. On the final day the goddess is feasted, propitiated with sacrifices, and entreated to move on east. When a goddess came through the land in the summer of 1965, only the hamlets of Konduru organized the proper rituals. The village itself had grown too large and lacked the strong leadership needed for the ceremonies. Some of the villagers arranged their own rites. The aged in Konduru recalled with nostalgia the days when all would have joined in the worship and when countless goats would have been sacrificed in the fields.

One of the more important village ceremonies is centered around the sacrifice of a young water buffalo in honor of the village goddess to engender village strength. While the ceremony has not been reported from the plateau since the late 1950s, it is still practiced, though infrequently, in the plains' villages nearby. On the night of the ceremony, the bull is beheaded with a single blow from the large sword of a Leather-worker. The entrails, head, and forefeet are taken with food sacrifices around the village boundaries. During the procession mantras are chanted, limes are cut and thrown into the air to dispel the demons (each being equal to the sacrifice of one human), and balls of rice mixed with blood are buried in the fields. Should an outsider later steal one of these balls, all the strength developed by the ceremonies would pass to his village; the thief then becomes the hero of his hometown. Tales persist of the Saranpur men who caught the Fine-Cloth Weaver who a few years back stole their offerings for Podur village. According to these tales the men beat him to within an inch of his life before taking back the food and letting him go. Other stories tell of daredevils who did not get away with their lives.

Village crisis rituals have a powerful integrative effect on the village. They unite different castes and different communities in concerted action to preserve the whole. Strong villages can unite in order to forestall disaster; weak ones can only bear their plagues in silence.

Rituals in Konduru provide families, castes, communities, and the village itself with visible symbols to show their solidarity and their place in the world, with relics to inspire their loyalties, with sacred myths to give them meanings, and with beliefs to defend.

CHAPTER EIGHT

THE CHANGING SCENE

ONE need only walk through the streets of Konduru to realize that change has been part of the village from its inception. Crumbling ruins and half-buried inscriptions which abound in and around Konduru testify to other times and scenes.

Bohannon notes (1963:369–71) that changes take place at different levels of the culture. Some rearrange the parts of a cultural system without altering the system itself. Others modify the parts of the system or even the system itself.

Historical fortunes, human aspirations, and external influences have generated tensions within the village in the past. Many of these have been resolved by readjustments within the village without seriously undermining its traditional patterns. Personal fortunes alter the roles of individuals and families. For instance, the Konduru Ramsetti family, once quite poor, now dominates the finance of the plateau. Whether the grandfather actually found a pot of gold as he claimed, or only used this story to justify wealth gained by trade is not important. What is clear is that while the Ramsettis were formerly paupers, they now command power and prestige. Likewise historical fortunes vary the positions of castes and social groups. Konduru Herdsmen, once powerful in the past, are now suffering from a plague of deaths. Believing themselves under a curse, they are leaving the village for the hamlets and other villages. The Weavers, on the other hand, have grown rapidly and were successful in their bid to take over the Rangapur temple from the Brahmans. However, such changes do not alter the basic structure of the village itself.

Far more fundamental changes have occurred in Konduru which have transformed or threatened to destroy its very nature. The coming of Islam and the Muslim states, the transformation from feudal jagirs to national government, and, more recently, the coming of Indian independence have all left their indelible imprints upon the face of the village. But while change has always been a part of the village, it would appear that Konduru is facing changes today at a rate unsurpassed in the past. Villagers, particularly the leaders, are aware that the structures which have served them for so long are being shaken.

CHANGES IN TECHNOLOGY

Technological change is obvious and all pervasive. Modern tools, cycles, watches, radios, buses, and trucks are common sights. Local merchants stock safety pins, lanterns, flashlights, soaps, gas lamps, galvanized buckets, kerosene, thread, needles, and factory-woven cloth. Women, for the most part, wear traditional dress, but progressive men are frequently seen in modern-style pants and shirts. Even a new Barber band with its modern instruments and tunes is replacing the old band.

Occupational monopolies have been variously affected by technological change. Some, notably the handicrafts, have been undermined by factory products. The Tailor caste had a monopoly over the hand stitching of cloth, but when sewing machines were introduced, they failed to extend these rights to the use of machines. Today men of other castes, notably the Muslims, have turned to tailoring, only to be threatened in turn by ready-made clothes brought to the weekly market from distant towns and cities. Weavers and Cottoncarders lost a large share of their work to gins and mills; Potters lost a considerable share to aluminum factories, and, almost a century ago, Gypsies lost their jobs as transporters to trains and trucks. Even the Ironsmiths and Carpenters, whose skills are needed for repairs and custom-crafted articles, find villagers turning to factory-made tools. Work monopolies, which still operate effectively as life moves into the last third of the twentieth century, exist for the menial services of washing clothes, cutting hair, sweeping, and leather work. To date these have not been breached by machines, but they are threatened by the breakdown of the patron-client systems in favor of contractual arrangements.

Changes in the occupational structure have not gone unchallenged. On the plateau, the Fine-Cloth Weavers have organized their caste along union lines in order to compete with factory products. By taking the initiative and establishing shops in villages such as Konduru, they have reintroduced handwoven cloth throughout the region. They standardized their products and thereby gained a reputation for producing durable cloth for everyday wear. While their homespun cannot compete with the fine factory cloths which carry status, it has a growing market in the village. On the other hand, the Konduru Winetappers are split by dissensions and, unlike some Winetappers of the plains, they have been unable to organize a caste union to exploit their occupation.

Modern technology has not only destroyed old jobs, but it has also given the village new ones. Cycles, trucks, modern medicine, and the like call for new specialists. New jobs in large towns or in the city attract Konduru men for varying periods of time. Some have returned, but many of the younger men have taken permanent jobs elsewhere.

Technological changes have also had a profound effect upon transportation and communications. The motorable road connecting Konduru to the external world was completed in the 1920s. Until then small plateau oxcarts with solid-wood wheels rattled along rough country trails. Even though today's plains-style oxcarts with large spoked wheels still are the backbone for local transportation, buses and trucks arrive daily connecting Konduru with the external world. Merchants trade in distant markets and truck back products for sale. Some villagers travel long distances to visit relatives, like Krishna Chari whose in-laws live in Mysore and the Tamil merchant who annually treks to Tamilnad. Other villagers go on bus tours to the great Hindu shrines of southern India. Twice in 1964 and again in 1965 scores of local folk left, on conducted tours, to see a dozen important temples as far south as Madras and Madura. For many of the devotees, the trip was a fulfillment of sacred vows to a god such as Venkateshvarudu at Tirupati. Today these distant Hindu shrines have become known to most of the villagers as the returnees tell their experiences again and again. Buses are still a luxury for most, but they have opened avenues of communication with the outside world from which new ideas arrive.

CHANGES IN GOVERNMENT

Konduru has lived under many governments, but those in the last century have differed in significant ways from earlier ones. In contrast to the decentralized and often limited nature of earlier systems, recent governments, influenced in part by British colonial rule, have been centralized, with control extending throughout the realm down to the level of the village. They have also been broad in scope. Government responsibility now includes education, maintenance of health and general welfare, and other functions previously left largely to villages and castes. Admittedly the currents of centralization and inclusiveness have flowed most swiftly in the regions of India under direct British control, but the princely state of Hyderabad was not sheltered from the tide. Pressured by a British resident and such outstanding leaders as the Salar Jungs, the Nizams gradually accepted, though sometimes grudgingly, changes which have dramatically altered the countryside. After the 1870s, railroads and roads were rapidly extended; statewide police and court systems were established; and government hospitals based on modern allopathic medicine, post offices, and schools and administrative centers were organized in towns and larger villages. After the coming of independence, the influx of ideas increased tremendously through the government channels of the Community Development Blocks, as well as through Naya Panchayats, village level workers, health programs of all types, mass education, adult literacy programs, and radio.

Not all ideas, by any means, have been accepted. Some, like the court system, have been reinterpreted by the village to fit its own power structures. But many new concepts have become a part of everyday life. Although modern medicine has been introduced by Christian missions and the state government, for many villagers it is just another avenue for seeking cures. There is no question of alternatives, since villagers are not opposed to using magical, herbal, and homeopathic systems along with modern medical aid. While many go to the mission hospital at Jadcherla, sixty miles away, for modern medicine, most go to the local government hospital and doctor. The villagers complain that the service is poor at times, and the doctor complains that the monthly supply of free drugs seldom lasts two weeks. Yet there is a growing trust in the new methods of treatment, particularly when a needle, which seems to have an aura of mystery about it, is used.

Public health programs such as malaria eradication and plague control combined with current medicines have markedly increased life expectancy and Konduru is feeling the pressures of population growth. In 1921 the population of the village with its hamlets was 4,084 and by 1961 it was 6,251. Other villages and hamlets on the plateau are experiencing the same growth. Since the surrounding forest reserve land has been closed to further agricultural development, the problems of population pressure and land fragmentation, which has been characteristic of plains' villages for some time, are now appearing in Konduru as well. Concepts of public health are having other effects: several plateau hamlets located in swampy lowlands have relocated on higher ground. For the new sites, straight streets are drawn checkerboard fashion and houses are constructed in the blocks. New wells are guarded by stone and cement walls.

Government schools are springing up rapidly on the plateau. Until the mid-twentieth century, the plateau had a single elementary public school located in Konduru, a small private Muslim school, and several Hindu gurus who taught children for a fee. Harijan children, for the most part, attended a Christian mission school in Nagerkurnool, or no school at all. Beginning in 1959, the government upgraded Konduru's public school until it had become a high school in 1963. Primary schools were established in thirty-five other villages and hamlets (thirty-two of these are one-teacher schools) on the plateau, and two more middle schools were opened. Today children from many castes join in classes. High-caste families, Muslims, and the large Harijan Weaver caste have taken advantage of the schools for their sons, and even a few girls from the upper castes attend schools. Shudra castes generally need their children to help carry on hereditary jobs.

The local school has become the image of modern progress for Konduru youth. Traditionally, education has been considered a prized treasure to be acquired by a trusted few. Students had to renounce the world and seek out a guru who tested each student to ascertain his worthiness. Such education often had no direct economic remuneration. Today the schools are open to all. In addition to education, the Konduru high school sponsors sports tournaments with other schools of the region, stages classical dramas on its porches, and observes national festivals on its grounds. Until recent days, the school and the Naya Panchayat office had the only radios in town.

Teachers symbolize for many the image of the new enlightened India, but their leadership is not unopposed, particularly by the aged and the tradition-oriented youth. When the teachers of Konduru organized a weekly *bajan* in the Rama temple, the young Merchant men started a rival *bajan* in the Shiva temple. Dramas presented by the teachers and students have little in common with the street plays enacted by the un-educated youths. What inroads education has made in the village come primarily through students and those teachers who are also members of the village itself. New ideas taught in the school find slow entrance into the home. Little caste discrimination is openly observable in the school grounds today. A few years ago, when the schools were opened, the Harijans sat apart. Now students mingle freely in the classrooms and on the playground. Sociograms administered in the Konduru high school show preferences for intimate friendships between members of the same community and more hostility between communities, but what is striking is the number of friendships between high-caste boys and Harijans and between Hindus and Muslims. But in the more traditional contexts of the village, interaction between these groups is more restrained. Con-cepts of ritual purity are reaffirmed as orthodox Brahman children pause in their foyers to take ceremonial baths and don clean clothes before entering the house.

Probably the greatest effect of education is literacy. Books and a half dozen copies of a daily Telugu newspaper bring to Konduru an aware-ness of the outside world. Visions of the external world are often strange mixtures of fact and fantasy, yet the awareness itself is a powerful influ-ence. Events close to home such as the Chinese invasion and the war with Pakistan are widely discussed, particularly by the educated and the young.

The Community Development programs introduced to the plateau in the past decade are more deliberate attempts on the part of the govern-ment to introduce widespread cultural change to the villages. Personnel, information, and financial assistance are sent out from the Community Block headquarters through such diverse schemes as agricultural devel-opment, cooperatives, youth associations, music, and handicrafts. While most of these projects are in the incipient stages and their effects are only beginning to be felt in Konduru, a few have already made deep impressions upon the world of the village. Under the dynamic leader-ship of a progressive Block Development officer, a program of self-help for the schools was carried out in 1964. Villagers competed in making donations of maps, pictures, clocks, and other educational equipment to their own schools. Equipment worth over seventeen thousand rupees was donated during a four-month period on the plateau. Other programs will have an even more profound effect upon the plateau in the near future. The extension of roads into the hinterland will open the doors for travelers and rapid import and export of commodities. Construction on a large dam near Shri Salem has already led to a new road through the forest from Maredpur to the dam site and, consequently, to a heavy flow of traffic across the end of the plateau. Local leaders hope that this dam will also bring electricity to Konduru.

The initiation of democratic processes and, more recently, the decentralization of power in the form of the Naya Panchayat are affecting the village power structure. Elections open new doors for winning and losing power and prestige. Whether achieved status will gradually replace ascribed status as the dominant organizing principle of the village, or whether new avenues will develop for converting newly acquired political power into the traditional ascribed systems of status remains to be seen. While Konduru elections, so far, have by and large reaffirmed the power of the old leaders, new ones of low-caste groups are beginning to exercise the power which their numerical superiority makes possible. So far they have been content to press for small gains while the powerful middle-ranked Reddis challenge the Brahman-Merchant power establishment.

CHANGING IDEAS

Changes in technology and massive governmental programs have markedly increased the flow of communication to Konduru. This communication brings in the new ideas which lie at the heart of any change. Today the pros and cons of human equality, personal freedom, and technological change are topics of lively discussion by men in the village square. When a foreigner is available, questions asked frequently concern the caste systems, marriage patterns, and economic conditions in the foreign lands. Men also discuss the growing interest in material gain. In the old days no houses were rented; they were loaned to the needy for their upkeep. Today, with government officers and outsiders in town, each empty house has its price. Even Harijan government workers from afar can rent houses amid the clean castes so long as they hire high-caste women to draw their water from the community well. Untouchability is gone in some of its more outward forms. Harijans who appear in the marketplace and on the buses need not take any note of caste segregation. Yet many ideas which are mentally accepted find slower translation into action. Despite laws to the contrary, Konduru's temples are in actual practice closed to the Harijans. Young men discuss cases of "love marriage," but these marriages are not common and almost never cross caste lines.

Maybe the greatest change in Konduru today lies in the general orientation of its generations. Old men lament the passing of a golden age in the past. For them changes are mixed blessings. Their feelings are summed up by the aged village philosopher, Goldsmith Lakshayya who wrote in part:

> Consider the times and compare,
>   Weakness is increasing everywhere.
> The walking child has returned to crawl,
>   In this age, O Kodanda Rama of Konduru.
>
> Man ignores the instructions of others,
>   Himself he cannot understand,
> Even God cannot remove his obstinacy,
>   The fish he caught was a whale, the
>   one he lost a minnow.
>
> The value of gold and silver has soared,
>   All have turned to imitations.
> Masters eat the food of the laborers,
>   Like men who eat the oxen with the crop.
>
> They think that only wealth is permanent,
>   They understand not the lessons of want.
> But wealth and want are both essentials in life,
>   O Thou, Kodanda Rama of Konduru.
>
> The son rejects his father's vocation,
>   The daughter-in-law disobeys her mother-in-law,
> All harmony and unity are gone,
>   In this world, O Kodanda Rama of Konduru.
>
> None reveres the saint of his own village,
>   All honor the cheat from afar,
> The neighbor's milk, though sour, tastes good,
>   In this world, O Kodanda Rama of Konduru.
>
> Yet you are silent as Bharata.
>   Will the godless remember you?
> Arise and judge the wicked,
>   O Thou, Kodanda Rama of Konduru.

Many in the younger generation, on the other hand, look to a utopia ahead. To them change itself is an accepted and desired way of life. More and more they look to the outside world for new ideas and to the tomorrow when these will be put into practice.

CHAPTER NINE

CONCLUSIONS

Is THE village a useful unit of analysis? Some men such as Henry Maine, Karl Marx, Mahatma Gandhi, Nilakanta Sastri, and T. V. Mahalingam have viewed villages as the ultimate building blocks of Indian society and, hence, the most significant units of analysis. Others such as Dumont (1957) and Pocock (1960) have denied the importance of the village and stressed that of caste. In recent years a more balanced approach has been reached (Dube, Lewis, Bailey, Marriott, Mandlebaum, etc.) in which the importance of the village as a social entity is recognized with the realization that there are other groups of equal significance in the Indian society.

Konduru illustrates the place of the village within the social order. At first glance the importance of the village is readily apparent — its borders are clearly marked, its inhabitants can be observed, and its activities charted. Yet further examination shows that other social groups are of equal or greater importance in the lives of the inhabitants. Such groups divide the village on the one hand, but on the other, by cutting across village boundaries, they bind men into relationships that stretch across the countryside. To the extent that attention is focused upon these other groups the form of the village becomes blurred.

The village cannot be understood apart from the other social groupings in which the villagers participate. A man finds his primary identification in groups based upon kinship and consciousness of kind. Within the circles of his family and local lineage he learns, as a child, the behavior patterns of his caste and society. He learns the importance and symbolism of pollution and purity, of hierarchy and power. Through his

167

elders he finds his primary support and his place within the world of caste. With relatives of his own age, among whom are his closest friends and bitterest enemies, he experiences his first struggles for power and prestige.

No less important are the ties of caste which provide a man with a circle of potential kin and associates. Fellow castemen provide him with brides and grooms for his children. They gather to celebrate with him the great ritual events of his life. Those in other villages provide him with a place to stay and vouch for him in his business dealings. But caste ties are more than potential and realized social bonds. They link men to people of their own culture and kind. A man feels at home with the values and behavior practices of his fellow castemen. He shares with them common interests in work, caste histories, caste deities, and the maintenance of cultural distinctives. With them he also competes for the power and respect of the caste.

The villager is also aware that he is a member of a society in which his caste is one among many and is dependent upon other castes for the performance of various essential tasks. As Bougle notes (Hutton 1963: 124), for Hindus patriotism consists in attachment to the caste system and they achieve the paradox of being unable to unite except in the very culture pattern that divides them. The caste system does more than provide order within a pluralistic society; it provides the individual with a place within it. A man obtains his primary status from his caste. The caste system also gives him a mental image of his society and world, a sort of social world view which has a sense of order and rightness about it. The values and norms that guide his behavior spring from this social ethos.

The influence of geography as a limiting factor upon social relationships cannot be ignored. A man does not live within the whole of his caste or society, but within those segments of caste and society with which he has contact. His face-to-face relationships are confined mainly to his community, his village, and the plateau.

The relationship between geography and the social order can be illustrated by an analysis of caste. Castes, in reality, exist as local caste groups which are linked in various ways with similar groups elsewhere. Within the local setting caste boundaries are defined, caste distinctions are defended, and caste offenses are punished. But villagers are linked by bonds of marriage, kinship, and association to local caste groups elsewhere, which in turn have ties to still other caste groups beyond. More-over, local caste groups in some castes are linked with similar castes in neighboring villages to form caste regions. A man thinks of his total caste largely in terms of his local and regional caste groups. To him it has a clearly defined membership and a definite place in society comparable to the place of his local caste group within his village society. The ana-lyst, however, must distinguish between mental images of the social order and social realities. He is aware that in fact caste boundaries are lost in the extension; that a caste, although united in one area, may be split in two in another; that the same caste may rank high in one region and low in another; and that a caste as a whole is a nebulous constella-tion of local caste groups rather than a corporate entity.

Like the villagers, early analysts appear at times to have failed to differentiate between castes as broad societal categories and castes as local groups. The confusion is not without some justification, for unlike American classes that as societal categories have no corresponding social groups (i.e., men do not join a "Middle Class Club" but a club having middle class status), Indian castes as societal categories do have roughly corresponding local groups (i.e., men belong to the general Weaver Caste and to the local Weaver Caste group). It becomes increasingly clear that one must differentiate between local caste groups, castes as a whole as perceived by villagers, and castes as wholes in actual operation. To the anthropologist, the most meaningful definition of caste begins with the delineation of the local caste groups and then works up through the various linkages between these to the villagers' mental image of their total society, rather than starting with a broad definition of caste within the Indian society and then working down to its application at the level of the village.

If it is true that the village cannot be understood apart from the other social groups in which its resident members participate, it is also true that these groups cannot be understood apart from the village, for it is on the level of the village that the essential segments of the society are articulated into an interactional whole. Not all castes are present in a village, but the nature and operation of the caste system can be observed. Not all social situations are found there, but those that can be observed provide us with an understanding of the structure and dynamics that integrate society. This does not deny the ties linking individuals and groups from different villages to each other or the unique relationships shared between whole villages and hamlets and villages elsewhere. For example, the residents of Konduru's hamlets refer to Konduru as their "mother village" in the same way that the Gypsy *tandas* of the plateau speak of the first *tanda* built on the plateau as their progenitor. But the village itself is the local cross-section of the total society.

The ability of a village to mirror the total society is partly a function of size. Hamlets and small villages are generally limited residence groups based upon agriculture, caste, power, or convenience. Because they do not provide within themselves all essential functions of a society, they are dependent upon neighboring villages for many of their services. Large villages with their many specialist castes are less dependent upon the outside world for basic services and, hence, reflect more clearly the complex nature of the society as a whole. Yet villages retain a sense of community: their inhabitants are generally acquainted with their fellow villagers and are aware of the major events taking place within the village. Towns and cities may be better examples of the complexity of the society, at least for the analyst, but their sheer size precludes their being experienced as single communities by their inhabitants, who find most of their face-to-face relationships confined to the neighborhoods and communities.

Konduru vividly portrays the social fragmentation of the society. Castes, subcastes, gotras, lineages, families, communities, political alliances and associations of many kinds separate men. Even the geographic distribution of people within the village reflects these divisions. Households contain members of families; particular streets and lanes are generally identified with members of particular lineages or small castes; and neighborhoods are often occupied by members of a single large caste. The untouchables live apart in separate enclaves or *pālems* near the village. Even the use of graveyards and the local stream reflects the caste divisions.

Konduru also portrays the stability of the caste society, a stability which has helped it to exist for at least seven centuries amid repeated crises and changes. This durability springs from several sources. First, the mobilization of human and natural resources by the caste system is such that there is a structured dependence between the parts. Castes rely upon each other for essential services and rituals, so much so that Furnival notes (Hutton 1963:128) "secession is identical with anarchy." In operation this dependence gives rise to networks such as jajmani and begar which link together specific families of different castes with economic and ritual ties. Moreover, within the system, relationships between men of different castes are structured by the principles of hierarchy and ritual purity which make interaction possible. This system finds its model and justification in the villager's religious world view.

In the second place, integration of the village society is achieved by the associations and alliances which cut across caste lines bridging the rifts between them by generating multiple loyalties. While such groups generally form within the major communities, there are certain all-village activities that bridge community differences.

A third integrative factor is found in the panchayats which resolve the conflicts that threaten the operation of the village. Workable solutions are found to disputes that arise within the multicultural society in which no single set of norms or code of law predominates and in which, on some occasions, there is no single dominant source of power.

Village panchayats play another equally significant role in the integration of the village. They provide a way to recognize changes in the social order without having to acknowledge that change has actually taken place. The process is illustrated by Pocock's observation (1960:69), "A caste, despite living memory of inferiority, was said to be of superior origin and therefore entitled to reassume its ancient position. By framing the decision in this manner change was formally denied while its results were at the same time ratified." Most castes have such stories of superior origins and others can be created for the occasion. The durability of the village is in no small measure dependent upon this social flexibility beneath an apparently rigid surface, a flexibility which reduces the tensions arising from the cultural lag between social structures and the social realities arising out of the historical vagaries of life.

In the fourth place integration is achieved through rituals. The formal cyclic rites of Konduru's high religions relate to various families, castes, and communities. Beneath these lies an awareness of the essential unity of the village in the face of external threat and crisis. Invading powers, whether divine or human, must be resisted or placated and sent on their way. In times of plague, famine, and crisis, the village goddess must be propitiated and village strength renewed at the Navel Stone. The supernatural defenses of the village must be renewed at its borders.

Finally, village solidarity rests, as Mandelbaum notes (Singer and Cohn 1968:42), upon common association. "Villagers live close to each other, see each other, and interact more frequently than they do with people of other villages. They share the same familiar life-space and share also common experiences of famine or harvest bounty, of flood or epidemic, of village fast or festivals."

In the world beyond his village, a man is identified with his village. Strangers first ask him where he comes from — caste status is inferred from signs on his body, his appearance, his ways of speaking, and his general demeanor. As one informant said, "If at first you ask a man about his caste the relationship breaks." Men who need someone to vouch for their integrity usually turn to fellow castemen in the village or to fellow villagers who may be in the vicinity.

The people of Konduru belong to many groups and the relationships between these are neither simple nor static. In the realities of daily life a man turns for identification and support first to one group, then to another, depending upon the occasion, the surrounding circumstances, and the personal designs of the individual. This enactment of life, for the most part, takes place within the context of the village which, for the individual, is the concrete expression of his society.

APPENDIXES, BIBLIOGRAPHY, AND INDEX

APPENDIXES

APPENDIX I. OCCUPATIONAL MONOPOLIES OF CASTES ON THE KONDURU PLATEAU

HINDU SEDENTARY CASTES

Brahmans
  Āndhra Smārthulu
    Vaidike   Village and family purohits
    Aruvēlu Niyōgis   Village patwari, land accountant
  Kanadi Sri Vaishnava
    Ayyavaru   Priest in Rama temple
Kshatriya (nonresident)
Vaishya
  Yēgina Kōmati   Merchants and moneylenders
Uncertain Varna
  Tambali   Lamplighters in Shiva temple
  Nambi   Lamplighters in Hanuman shrine
Vishva Brahmans
  Ausali   Goldsmiths
  Kamari   Ironsmiths
  Vadla   Carpenters
  Kansari   Brass-smiths
Shudras
  Reddis   Farmers
  Kamma Kāpu   Farmers
  Munnur   Farmers
  Māden   Farmers
  Gādzalu   Braceletmakers
  Sanchi Pūsali   Door-to-door salesmen
  Telugu   Gatherers of forest fruits
  Darji or Māra   Tailors
  Sāle   Weavers of fine cloth
  Kummari   Potters
  Bondili   Peons and bodyguards
  Bhat Raj   Bards and traders
  Bhoi or Bēsta   Fishermen
  Bōgam   Courtesans and dancing girls
  Golla   Herdsmen

175

Kuruva	Herdsmen and blanket weavers
Gaundlu	Winetappers
Sevak or Chapka	Servants
Biksha	Dramatists and beggars
Mangali	Barbers, surgeons, musicians
Tsākali or Dhōbi	Washermen
Harijans	
Māla	
Dāsari	Mala gurus and priests
Māla	Weavers and sweepers
Pamblewad	Mala musicians
Madiga	
Baine	Madiga priests
Madiga	Leatherworkers
Marginal Castes and Tribes	
Deva Chenchu	Forest Chenchu tribesmen
Grāma Chenchu	Village Chenchu tribesmen
Lambardi	Gypsies and herdsmen

HINDU TRANSIENT CASTES

Symbiotic Castes	
Pagateshagāndlu	Put on masks and beg at homes of Merchants, Reddis, and Brahmans; hunt small game with dogs; repair drums
Mailalu	Priests to the Merchants, using brass masks of the gods, a triangle, and bells
Viramushti	Beggars and acrobats to the Merchants
Dzalugari	Bring sand for Goldsmiths and take the used sand from which they extract gold spillings in payment
Pitsakuntla	Bards and historians to Kapu and Golla, manufacture pedigrees, herbal doctors
Podapātra	Dramatists to the Golla Herdsmen
Adep Sing	Historians and beggars to the Barbers
Māla Māshti	Harijan acrobats and entertainers for the Weavers
Mādiga Māshti	Harijan acrobats and entertainers for the Leatherworkers
Sindu	Harijan courtesans and entertainers for the Leatherworkers
Dakkali	Beggars to the Leatherworkers
Priests, Entertainers, and Beggars	
Budubudukalu	Professional beggars and mantrakars
Tsākali Budubudukalu	Magicians, snake charmers, ropemakers
Tūrka Budubudukalu	Beggars to Muslims; rouse Muslims to eat before dawn during Ramzan
Kātipāpulu	Beggars
Bālasantālu	Beggars with a horn and bell
Tōluboppala	Leather puppeteers
Linga Balija	Shiva mendicants and herbal doctors
Mutrāsi	Watchmen and minstrels
Dēvara	Beggars with boxes of small idols of Kanika Durgamma, whip themselves to arouse sympathy

Gangedulu	Mendicants with sacred bulls which they cause to perform for alms
Bālasantālu	Entertainers of children and singers
Mushti	Priests of Shiva and fortune-tellers
Arakartikevaru	Beggars with small stringed instruments
Garnātulum	Bards at Shudra homes
Are Baine	Palmists and storytellers
Koya Chenchu	Beggars with silver masks and peacock feathers, sell bear and tiger medicines
Dommara	Jugglers, tumblers, tightrope dancers and prostitutes, hunt small game and make medicines for hernia, rheumatism, etc., and treat these by sucking through a cow's horn
Gāradi	Snake charmers, magicians, and slight of hand artists
Mondi	Ruined caste whose members have the right to take any wife with a nose or ear that has been disfigured by an angry husband

Traveling Salesmen and Craftsmen

Gāndlavāru	Oil extractors
Telagālam	Salesmen of small jewelry
Mēdari	Basketweavers, weavers of mats
Artukarivāru	Weavers of large bamboo screens
Patkarivāru	Sellers of silk and expensive cloth
Perikivāru	Traders in salt and grain

Semitribal Castes

Erakala	Soothsayers, fortune-tellers, pig herders, hunters of small game; there are three divisions
Kāsha	Makers of grindstones at the quarries near Tartikol, present from August to November; Quarrymen
Uppari	Earthmovers, diggers of wells, builders of walls, roads, and dams
Vadda	Rock crushers and rock extractors

MUSLIM CASTES

Arabs	Muslims who trace their ancestry back to Arabia
Turka	Major Muslim caste with four subdivisions: Sayeds, Sheikhs, Mogals, and Patans; no Patans are found on the plateau
Fakir	Muslim mendicants and entertainers
Tōla	Handlers of sheepskins
Dudēkulu	Cottoncarders; probably of Hindu origin and retain most Hindu customs

APPENDIX II. SUPERNATURAL BEINGS OF THE KONDURU HINDU COMMUNITY

COMMON DEITIES OF HINDUISM WORSHIPED IN KONDURU

GODS OF THE HINDU GREAT TRADITION

Vishnu: one of the Hindu triad and worshiped in his incarnations as *Narasimha*, half man and half lion, and as *Rāma*. In the latter form he is associated with *Laxmana*, his brother, and *Sīta*, his wife. *Lakshmi* and *Sarasvati*, his consorts, are also worshiped.

Shiva or *Ishvarudu*: god of destruction or absorption in the Hindu triad, with *Nandi* his vehicle.

Ganesh or *Ganapati* or *Vināyaka*: the elephant-headed god who has the mouse as his vehicle. *Subramanya* or *Karttikēya* his brother who rides the peacock is also worshiped.

Hanuman or *Anjanēlu*: the monkey-faced god who assisted Rama. He is worshiped in his own shrine in the fierce form.

Venkatēshvarudu: a form of Vishnu worshiped by high castes. Temples at Tirupathi and Palem are popular pilgrimages for local folk. This god was claimed by the Konduru Weavers who have his shrine beyond Konduru.

Mallikarjuna: a form of Shiva enshrined in the Konduru Weaver temple and in Shri Salem.

Kāli: the fierce and bloody consort of Shiva.

Tulsi Tree: sacred to Brahmans and Merchants.

Agni: fire used in human worship.

Sūrya and *Chendrudu*: sun and moon. Brahmans revere the sun daily in the Gayatri mantra.

Nandi: the cow, honored at Chiluka Duvadasi.

GODS OF THE REGIONAL AND LOCAL TRADITIONS

Jamavantudu: Leatherworker caste god, claimed by them to be oldest of all gods.

Chenikēshvarudu: god of Rayalgundi traditionally worshiped by Weavers.

Malikēshvarudu: popular god enshrined in forest near Lalapur.

Bālāji: god of the Gypsy caste.

Lingamayya: god of the Chenchu and the forest. Loosely linked to Shiva.

Jami Tree and *Banyan Tree*: common sites of worship.

Krishna River and mountains: rivers such as the Krishna and Ganges and some mountains are objects of worship.

DEITIES OF THE KONDURU LOW RELIGION

THE SEVEN SISTERS

Pōshamma: also known as Polaramma, Polkamma, Annamma, and Muthyalamma. Goddess of smallpox, stomachaches, and many illnesses. Formerly Konduru had a large festival in her honor with the Baine or a Washerman as priest.

Pedamma: loosely identified with Kalika Devi. Goddess of the forest tigers who kill grazing cattle. Herdsmen used to hold periodic festivals at her shrine on the western edge of the village. The Baine and Leatherworkers have certain rights in her worship ceremony.

Yellamma: goddess of blindness, cholera, and sores. She grants offspring to the barren. She is enshrined near Tartikol but her "sight" reaches thirty miles so local folk attend her shrine regularly.

Bālamma: goddess who causes abortions, infant deaths, and lack of mother's milk.

Maicamma: goddess of accidents and diseases. Her forms include *pala maicamma*,

178

Milk Maicamma; *raktha maicamma*, Bloody Maicamma; *uppali maicamma*, Ferocious Maicamma; *kota maicamma*, Fort Maicamma, which requires buffalo sacrifices at the building of a fort; and *mēdarivarla maicamma*, Maicamma who possesses people.

Ēdamma: goddess who kills children and "pulls out the foundations of the home." Worshiped also by the Chenchu.

Mankārlamma: goddess worshiped particularly by the Brassworkers.

Potha Razu: younger brother of the seven sisters and their guardian.

OTHER GODS AND GODDESSES OF KONDURU

Sandla Saudamma: "In her sight lies buried treasure," goes the proverb. She stands on one foot and anyone who can figure out the meaning of her elusive gaze can find buried wealth.

Pinamma: goddess of Washermen. Propitiated by them in special rites.

Kanika Dūrgamma: goddess enshrined east of Konduru.

Gangamma: goddess of wells and rivers. Demands grain at harvesttime.

Bhavanamma: goddess of aches and pains. Found in Konduru and in several of the hamlets.

Vēranāgamma: goddess of headaches and infant deaths. Enshrined in Konduru homes.

Lakshmi: popular goddess also found in Hinduism. Takes three forms: *dhana lakshmi*, goddess of wealth, worshiped by Merchants and the rich; *doddi lakshmi*, goddess of cattle sheds, worshiped by herders; and *bhū lakshmi*, goddess of the earth, worshiped by farmers.

Savaramma: goddess enshrined east of Konduru and in the homes of Leatherworkers.

Nāgamma: goddess of the cobras.

Dūrgamma: goddess of power and destruction associated with *shakti*. She stands over the slain buffalo demon.

Kāli: the four-armed goddess.

Madel: god of the Washermen.

Bayanna: god of the forest Chenchu.

Narsappa: fierce demon placated by Hindus and Muslims.

SPIRITS AND POWERS OF THE LOW RELIGION

Bord Rayi: village Navel Stone, established at its founding.

Shakti: supernatural power, worshiped in its own right.

Kanikelu: supernatural beings of both sexes resident in some surrounding wells, fierce looking.

Rākshasas, Dayamulu, Gāli: demons, devils, wind. These are occasionally named though not sharply differentiated. Names include: Pulamma, Sītamma, Venkamma, Lingamma, Narajuramma, Jangamma, Parvathamma, Kankamma, Venkatamma, Kishtamma, Padmamma, Chendrakārlamma, Sesirēkamma, and others.

APPENDIX III. IMPORTANT HINDU MARRIAGE RITES OBSERVED BY VARIOUS CASTES IN KONDURU

Kottanam: Five women whose husbands are living prepare rice flour and powdered turmeric for use in the wedding by pounding them in a mortar with two wooden pestles which have been bound together and decorated with leaves.

Araveni kundalu: The ceremonial fetching of earthen pots from the home of the family potter. A procession goes to the home of the potter and offers rice, gram, and other foods to the pots which are then taken to the site of the wedding. Two large pots are decorated or painted white and are filled with water which has small lighted lamps floating on it. Smaller pots are brought for other ceremonial uses and for the feast.

Vāra nischaya: Worship of the village goddess. Food, clothing, betel leaves, and areca nuts are offered to different local goddesses. Goats or chickens may be sacrificed as well.

Prathānam: Preparation of the bride for the ceremonies in her home. The groom's parents and relatives bring gifts of coconut, betel, and the *prathan* ring to the bride's house. She is bathed and dressed. Seated on a low wooden stool she worships Ganesh and the ring brought from the groom.

Edurukolu: Meeting of the two kin groups prior to the wedding is described in the text.

Ghatikapūja: The bride and groom are bathed in turmeric. Some worship the Araveni pot at this time.

Madhuparka: A mixture of honey and ghee is given to the groom who is seated on a low stool at the marriage site. The Merchants invest the young man with the sacred thread at this time.

Lagnam: The bride is brought and seated opposite the groom with a cloth hung between them. Mantras are recited by the priest and rice sprinkled upon them by attendant priests and the audience.

Jilkerabellum (Jira gudam): The bride and groom throw cumin seed and jaggery on each other and the cloth screen is removed.

Padghattam: the bride and groom tread upon each other's feet.

Kanyadan: The gift of the virgin. Among the Merchants the bride's mother pours water into the hands of her husband from where it trickles down through the hands of the bride, and then through the groom's other hand and onto the plate below. Among some lower castes the bride's parents wash the feet of the groom and offer him honey, curds, and ghee. This ceremony symbolizes the presentation of the girl by her father as a gift to the groom.

Kankan visarjan: The bride's wrist threads are untied.

Uppagintha: The bride is formally entrusted by the parents to the charge of the husband and his kin who are requested to treat her kindly.

Barat: The bridal procession takes the groom with his new wife to the house of the groom.

BIBLIOGRAPHY

Ali, M. C., 1885. *Hyderabad under Sir Salar Jung.* 4 vols. Bombay: Education Society Press.

Allchin, A. R., 1963. *Neolithic Cattle-keepers of South India.* Cambridge: Cambridge University Press.

Bailey, F. G., 1960. *Tribe, Caste and Nation.* Bombay: Oxford University Press.

Basham, A. L., 1954. *The Wonder That Was India.* New York: Macmillan Co.

Beals, A. R., 1962. *Gopalpur, a South Indian Village.* New York: Holt, Rinehart and Winston.

Beidelman, T. O., 1959. *A Comparative Analysis of the Jajmani System.* New York: J. J. Augustin Inc.

Berreman, G. D., 1960. "Caste in India and the United States." *The American Journal of Sociology,* 66:120–127.

Beteille, Andre, 1965. *Caste, Class and Power: Changing Patterns of Stratification in a Tanjore Village.* Berkeley: University of California Press.

Bhagāyya, Chervirāla, 1962. *Anubhava Mantra Shāstramu.* Secunderabad: Konda Verayya and Sons.

Bhowmick, K. C., 1963. "Caste and Service in a Bengal Village." *Man in India,* 43:277–327.

Bierstedt, R., 1957. *Social Order: An Introduction to Sociology.* New York: McGraw-Hill Co.

Bilgrami, S. H., and C. Willmott, 1883. *Historical and Descriptive Sketch of His Highness, the Nizam's Dominions.* Bombay: Times of India Steam Press.

Bohannon, Paul, 1963. *Social Anthropology.* New York: Holt, Rinehart and Winston.

Carstairs, G. M., 1967. *The Twice-Born.* Bloomington: Indiana University Press.

Cohn, B. S., 1959. "Some Notes on Law and Change in North India." *Economic Development and Cultural Change,* 8:79–93. 1961. "From Indian Status to British Contract." *Journal of Economic History,* 21:613–628.

Coser, Lewis, 1964. *The Functions of Social Conflict.* Glencoe, Illinois: Free Press of Glencoe.

Devanandan, P. D., 1960. *The Changing Pattern of Family in India.* Bangalore: The Christian Institute for Study of Religion and Society.

Dey, S. K., 1962. *Panchayat Raj.* Bombay: Asia Publishing House.

Dixon, W. J., and F. J. Massey, 1957. *Introduction to Statistical Analysis.* New York: McGraw-Hill Co.

Dube, S. C., 1955a. *Indian Village.* London: Routledge and Kegan Paul.

———, 1955b. "Ranking of Castes in Telangana Villages." *The Eastern Anthropologist,* 8:182–190.

181

————, 1960. *India's Changing Villages: Human Factors in Community Development*. London: Routledge and Kegan Paul.

Dumont, Louis, 1957. "Village Studies." *Contributions to Indian Sociology*, 1:23–41.

Dutt, N. K., 1931. *Origin and Growth of Caste in India*. Vol. I. London: Kegan Paul, Trench, Trubner and Co.

Elmore, W. T., 1925. *Dravidian Gods in Modern Hinduism: A Study of the Local and Village Deities of Southern India*. Madras: Christian Literature Society.

Epstein, T. S., 1962. *Economic Development and Social Change in South India*. Bombay: Oxford University Press.

Evans-Pritchard, E. E., 1956. *Nuer Religion*. Oxford: Clarendon Press.

Foster, C. M., 1965. "Peasant Society and the Image of Limited Good." *American Anthropologist*, 67:293–315.

Freed, Stanley A., 1963. "An Objective Method for Determining the Collective Caste Hierarchy of an Indian Village." *American Anthropologist*, 65:879–891.

Fürer-Haimendorf, C. von, 1943. *The Chenchu: The Aboriginal Tribes of Hyderabad*. London: Macmillan and Co. Ltd.

————, 1945. *Tribal Hyderabad*. Hyderabad: Revenue Department of the Government of H. E. H. the Nizam.

Gafoor, S. K. A., 1952. *Tribes and Tribal Welfare in Hyderabad*. Hyderabad: Government Press.

Gargi, Balwant, 1966. *Folk Theater of India*. Seattle: University of Washington Press.

Gluckman, Max, 1955. *The Judicial Process among the Barotse of Northern Rhodesia*. Glencoe, Illinois: The Free Press.

Gould, H. A., 1958. "Hindu Jajmani System: A Case of Economic Particularism." *Southwestern Journal of Anthropology*, 14:428–437.

————, 1964. "A Jajmani System of North India, Its Structural Magnitude and Meaning." *Ethnology*, 3:12–41.

Government of Andhra Pradesh, 1957. *Supplement to Manual on Community Development*. Hyderabad: Planning and Development Department.

————, 1959. *District Statistical Handbook, 1950–51 to 1954–55: Mahbubnagar*. Hyderabad: The Bureau of Economics and Statistics, Planning and Development Department.

————, 1960. *Third Five-Year Plan*. Hyderabad: Planning and Local Administration Department.

————, 1962a. *Andhra Pradesh Panchayat Samithis and Zilla Parishads Act, 1959*. Hyderabad: Director, Government Press.

————, 1962b. *State Administration Report, 1960–61*. 2 vols. Hyderabad: General Administration Department.

————, 1962c. *Andhra Pradesh Village Panchayats Act of 1962*. Hyderabad: Director, Government Press.

————, 1966. *Census of India, 1961: District Census Handbook: Mahbubnagar District*. Hyderabad: Director, Government Press.

Government of Hyderabad, [1921?]. *Village List: 1921 Census*. Hyderabad: Government Press.

————, 1954. *Some Aspects of Hyderabad*. Hyderabad: Department of Information and Public Relations.

————, 1955. *Census of India, 1951: District Census Handbook: Mahbubnagar District, Part II*. Hyderabad: Bureau of Economics and Statistics.

Government of India, 1960. *Report of the Committee on Special Multipurpose Tribal Blocks*. New Delhi: Ministry of Home Affairs.

————, 1962. *Report of the Study Team on Naya Panchayats, April, 1962*. New Delhi: General Manager, Government of India Press.

Gribble, J. D. B., 1886. *Two Native States: Being Letters from Hyderabad and Mysore*. Madras: Lawrence Asylum Press.

————, 1896. *A History of the Deccan.* Vol. I. London: Luzac and Co.

Gupt, Nagabhushanam, 1958. *Sri Vasavekanyaka.* Secunderabad: Chandanarayarna Srashti.

Haranatrayya, K. C., 1964, *Shri Krodhināmasamvathsara Siddhāntha Koski Panchangam.* Secunderabad.

Harper, E., and W. Neals, 1959. "Two Systems of Economic Exchange in Village India." *American Anthropologist,* 61:760–778.

Hassan, S. S., 1920. *The Castes and Tribes of H. E. H. the Nizam's Dominions.* Bombay: Times Press.

Hiebert, P. G., 1969. "Caste and Personal Rank in an Indian Village: An Extension in Techniques." *American Anthropologist,* 71:434–453.

Hoebel, E. A., 1954. *The Law of Primitive Man: A Study of Comparative Legal Dynamics.* Cambridge, Mass.: Harvard University Press.

Hsu, F. L. K., 1963. *Clan, Caste and Club.* Princeton: Van Nostrand Co.

Husain, Mazhar, 1939. *Statistical Yearbook: 1345 Fasli (A.D. 1936).* Hyderabad: Government Central Press.

————, 1940. *Hyderabad District Gazetteers: Mahbubnagar, Tables Volume, 1340 and 1345 Fasli (A.D. 1931–1936).* Hyderabad: Government Central Press.

————, 1946. *Statistical Yearbook for 1350 Fasli (A.D. 1941).* Hyderabad: Government Central Press.

Hutton, J. H., 1963. *Caste in India.* 4th ed. Bombay: Oxford Press.

Iyengar, K. S., 1951. *Rural Economic Enquiries in the Hyderabad State, 1949–51.* Hyderabad: Government Press.

Jain, D. C., 1929. *Indigenous Ranking in India.* London: Macmillan and Co. Ltd.

Jouveau-Dubreuil, G., 1920. *An Ancient History of the Deccan.* Translated from the French by V. S. Swaminadha Dikshitar. Pondicherry: 6 Dumas Street.

Karve, Irawati, 1961. *Hindu Society, An Interpretation.* Poona: Deccan College.

————, 1965. *Kinship Organization in India.* 2nd ed. Bombay: Asia Publishing House.

Keesing, F. M., 1966. *Cultural Anthropology, The Science of Custom.* New York: Holt, Rinehart and Winston.

Ketkar, S. V., 1909. *History of Caste in India.* Vol. I. Ithaca, N.Y.: Taylor and Carpenter.

Kolenda, P., 1963. "Toward a Model of the Hindu Jajmani System." *Human Organization,* 22:11–31.

Lakshayyachari, 1951. *Vēdārnavanavanētamanu Gurusesya Samvādamu.* Secunderabad: Konda Shankarayya Premier Printers.

Leach, E. R., 1960. *Aspects of Caste in South India, Ceylon and North West Pakistan.* Cambridge: Cambridge University Press.

Lewis, Oscar, 1958. *Village Life in Northern India.* New York: Random House.

Llewellyn, K. N., and E. A. Hoebel, 1941. *The Cheyenne Way: Conflict and Case Law in Primitive Jurisprudence.* Norman: University of Oklahoma Press.

Lohia, Rammanohar, 1964. *The Caste System.* Hyderabad: Navahind.

Mahar, P. M., 1959. "A Multiple Scaling Technique for Caste Ranking." *Man in India,* 39:127–147.

Majumdar, D. N., 1958. *Caste and Communication in an Indian village.* Bombay: Asia Publishing House.

Mandelbaum, D. G., 1968. "Family, Jāti, Village." In M. Singer and B. S. Cohn (Eds.), *Structure and Change in Indian Society.* Chicago: Aldine Publishing Co.

Marriott, McKim (Ed.), 1955. *Village India: Studies in the Little Community.* Chicago: University of Chicago Press.

Marriott, McKim, 1960. *Caste Ranking and Community Structure in Five Regions of India and Pakistan.* Deccan College Monograph Series 23. Poona, India.

————, 1968. "Caste Ranking and Food Transactions: A Matrix Analysis." In

M. Singer and B. S. Cohn (Eds.), *Structure and Change in Indian Society.* Chicago: Aldine Publishing Co.

Mathur, K. S., 1964. *Caste and Ritual in a Malwa Village.* Bombay: Asia Publishing House.

Mayer, A. C., 1956. "Some Hierarchical Aspects of Caste." *Southwestern Journal of Anthropology,* 12:117–144.

———, 1960. *Caste and Kinship in Central India.* Berkeley: University of California Press.

Miller, E. J., 1954. "Caste and Territory in Malabar." *American Anthropologist,* 56:410–420.

Minturn, L., and J. T. Hitchcock, 1966. *The Rajputs of Khalapur, India.* New York: John Wiley and Sons.

Mirza, K., 1937. *A Brief Outline of the Geological History of Hyderabad State with a Reference to Its Mineral Resources.* Hyderabad: Government Press.

Moreland, W. H. (Ed.), 1931. *Relations of Golconda in the Early 17th Century.* London: Hakluyt Society.

Moulvie, S. M. A., 1889. *Hyderabad Affairs.* Bombay: Times of India Press.

Munshi, K. M., 1962. *Temples and Legends of Andhra Pradesh.* Bombay: Bharatiya Vidya Bhavan.

Murdock, G. P., 1965. *Culture and Society.* Pittsburgh: University of Pittsburgh Press.

Olsen, M. E., 1968. *The Process of Social Organization.* New York: Holt, Rinehart and Winston.

Orans, Martin, 1968. "Maximizing in Jajmaniland: A Model of Caste Relations." *American Anthropologist,* 70:875–897.

Orenstein, H., 1962. "Exploitation or Function in the Interpretation of Jajmani." *Southwestern Journal of Anthropology,* 18:302–316.

Pocock, D. F., 1960. "Sociologies — Urban and Rural." *Contributions to Indian Sociology,* 4:63–81.

———, 1962. "Notes on Jajmāni Relationships." *Contributions to Indian Sociology,* 6:78–95.

Rao, A. V. R., 1954. *Structure and Working of Village Panchayats.* Poona: Gokhale Institute of Politics and Economics.

Rapson, E. J. (Ed.), 1922. *The Cambridge History of India.* 6 vols. New York: Macmillan Co.

Retzlaff, R. H., 1962. *Village Government in India.* Bombay: Asia Publishing House.

Risley, H. H., 1891. *Tribes and Castes of Bengal.* 4 vols. Calcutta: Bengal Secretariat Press.

Rowe, W. L., 1963. "Changing Rural Class Structure and the Jajmani System." *Human Organization,* 22:41–44.

Roy, S. C., [n. d.]. *Caste, Race and Religion in India.* Ranchi: Man in India Office.

Rudolph, Lloyd I. and Susanne H. Rudolph, 1967. *The Modernity of Tradition: Political Development in India.* Chicago: University of Chicago Press.

Ryder, A. W. 1949. *The Panchatantra.* Bombay: Jaico Publishing House.

Saraswati, B., 1963. "Caste, Craft and Change." *Man in India,* 43:218–224.

Scott, J., 1794. *Ferishta's History of the Dekkan.* 2 vols. Shrewsbury: J. and W. Eddowes.

Senart, E., 1930. *Caste in India: The Facts and the System.* Translated from the French by E. Denison Ross. London: Methuen.

Siegel, Sidney, 1956. *Nonparametric Statistics for the Behavioral Sciences.* New York: McGraw-Hill Co.

Singer, Milton, 1959. *Traditional India: Structure and Change.* Philadelphia: American Folklore Society.

Singer, Milton and B. S. Cohn (Eds.), 1968. *Structure and Change in Indian Society.* Chicago: Aldine Publishing Co.

Spencer, R. F. (Ed.), 1954. *Method and Perspective in Anthropology*. Minneapolis: University of Minnesota Press.

Sreenivasachar, P. (Ed.), 1942. *A Corpus of Inscriptions in the Telingana Districts of H. E. H. the Nizam's Dominions*. 3 vols. Calcutta: H. E. H. the Nizam's Government.

Srinivas, M. N., 1952. *Religion and Society among the Coorgs of South India*. Oxford: Clarendon Press.

————, 1960. *India's Villages*. Bombay: Asia Publishing House.

Srinivas, M. N. and A. Beteille, 1964. "Networks in Indian Social Structure." *Man*, 64:165–168.

Stevenson, H. N. C., 1954. "Status Evaluation in the Hindu Caste System." *Journal of the Royal Anthropological Institute*, 84:45–65.

Temple, R., 1885. *Journals Kept in Hyderabad, Kashmir, Sikkim and Nepal*. Vol. 1. London: W. H. Allen and Co.

Thurston, E., 1909. *Castes and Tribes of Southern India*. 7 vols. Madras: Government Press.

Unnithan, T. K. N., Indra Deva, and Yogendra Singh (Eds.), 1965. *Towards a Sociology of Culture in India*. New Delhi: Prentice-Hall of India Ltd.

United States Department of Commerce, National Bureau of Standards, 1950. *Tables of the Binomial Probability Distribution*. Applied Mathematics, Ser. 6. Washington, D.C.: U.S. Government Printing Office.

Venkateshvaraswami, 1964. *Shrī Krōddhināma Samhra Sidhāntha Panchāngam*. Secunderabad: Dāchēpalli Kishtayya and Sons Printers.

Vīrabhadra, Mundūru, 1958. *Vāsthuchandrika*. Rajamandri, A.P., India: Karlahaste Tammaravu and Sons.

Whitehead, H., 1921. *The Village Gods of South India*. Calcutta: Association Press.

Wiser, W. H., 1936. *The Hindu Jajmani System*. Lucknow: Lucknow Publishing House.

Wiser, W. H. and C. V. Wiser, 1966. *Behind Mud Walls 1930–1960*. Berkeley: University of California Press.

Yazdani, G. (Ed.), 1960. *The Early History of the Deccan*. 2 vols. London: Oxford University Press.

INDEX

Achampet, 6, 36, 41, 49. *See also* Community Development Block, Samiti
Adep Sing, 41
Adoptive marriage, 34. *See also* Ilitum
Adultery, 105, 110, 111, 119
Agriculture, 6–8, 85–88
Alliances, 71, 72, 106, 170. *See* Caste
Anata Chaturdasi, 153
Andhra Pradesh, 126
Antapāt, 148
Arabs, 10, 29
Area councils (samitis), 78–79, 126
Artisan caste cluster. *See* Panchala
Āshrams (retreat center), 43
Associations, 40–44. *See* Social Structure
Astrology, 32, 115, 145, 150, 152
Aurangzeb, 10
Ayyavaru Brahmans (Shri Vaishnavas), 19, 70

Bahmanīs, 10
Baine, 26
Bajana, 40–41, 43, 44, 132, 134, 151, 163
Balachakravarthi, 152
Balaji, 135
Balija, 21, 22
Bands, 42–43, 87
Barbers, 41, 42, 62: history of, 10, 90–91; cases involving, 39, 70, 79, 91, 107, 110, 114–116; residence of, 46; alliances and rivalries of, 62, 75, 77, 78; jajmani network of, 87, 89, 148, 150; begar, 92–94; organization of, 120
Bards, 8, 22–23

Begar network, 81, 92–94, 171
Beggars, 25, 28, 74, 94
Berrygatherers, 24, 29, 45, 47, 48–49, 93
Biriki, 35
Birth, 25, 32, 58, 94–95, 111–112, 150
Bord rayi. See Navel stone
Braceletmakers, 22
Brahma, 134
Brahmans, 26, 41, 58, 82, 159, 164: as priests, 14, 20, 25, 34, 92, 114, 134, 135–136, 138, 145, 148, 152; place of in varna system, 14, 17; as gurus, 20, 27, 33; rites of, 21, 44, 52; history of, 22; marriage of, 22, 23, 25; cases involving, 23, 77–79; as village headmen, 64–65; alliances and rivalries among, 71, 75, 77–78; festivals of, 153
Brass-smiths, 17
Buffalo sacrifice, 123–124
Burial grounds, 53
Buried treasure, 143–145, 159

Carpenters: residence of, 46; occupation of, 84, 160; jajmani of, 86, 89, 150; begari of, 92, 94
Case studies of: lost work rights, 39; trespassing Washerman, 40; Konduru saint, 43; powerless Muslims, 71; rival politicians, 74–75; fight between the Weavers and Leatherworkers, 75–76; Konduru elections, 77–79; Barbers and the well, 79; coming of the Washermen and the Barbers, 90–91; death of the Gypsy creditor, 96; borrowed seed, 97; indentured